The Bhagavad-Gita
A Fresh Approach

Rajiv Sachdev **Karan Ahuja** **Neeraj Gupta**

STERLING

Bhagavad-Gita Study Should Be Started from a Tender Age

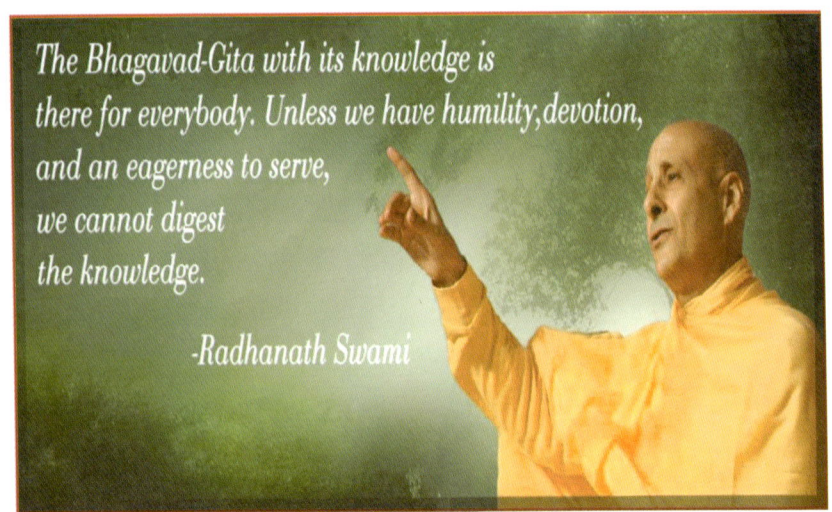

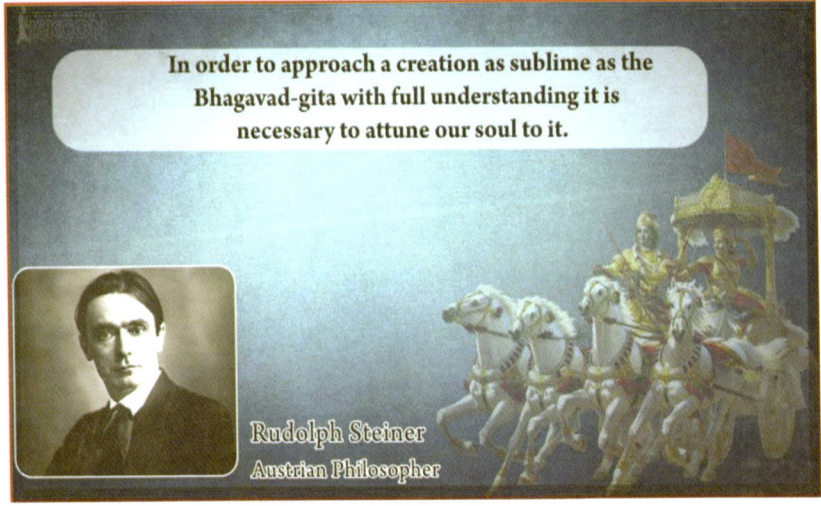

Bhagavad-Gita as Seen by the Learned Scholars and Rishis

When I read the Bhagavad-Gita and reflect about how God created this universe everything else seems so superfluous

— *Albert Einstein* —

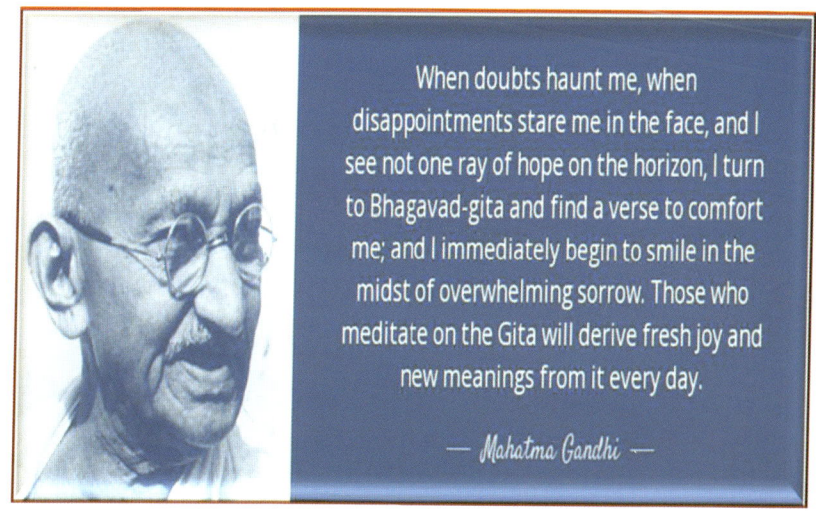

When doubts haunt me, when disappointments stare me in the face, and I see not one ray of hope on the horizon, I turn to Bhagavad-gita and find a verse to comfort me; and I immediately begin to smile in the midst of overwhelming sorrow. Those who meditate on the Gita will derive fresh joy and new meanings from it every day.

— *Mahatma Gandhi* —

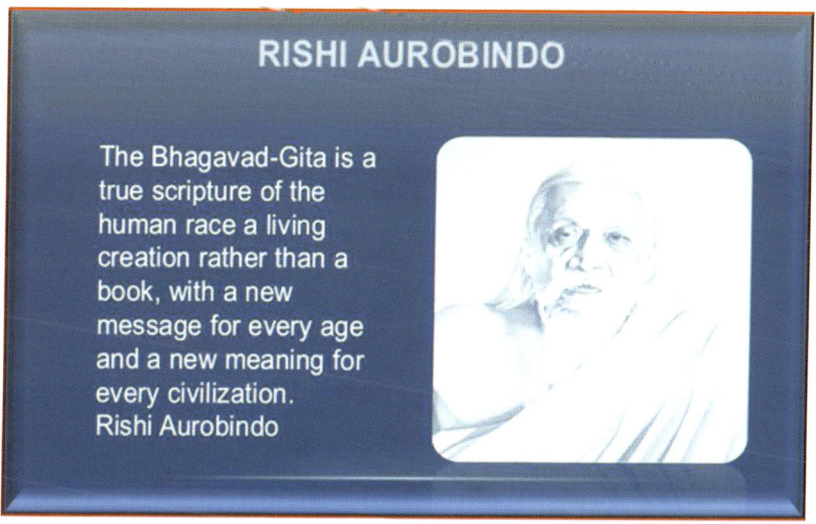

RISHI AUROBINDO

The Bhagavad-Gita is a true scripture of the human race a living creation rather than a book, with a new message for every age and a new meaning for every civilization.
Rishi Aurobindo

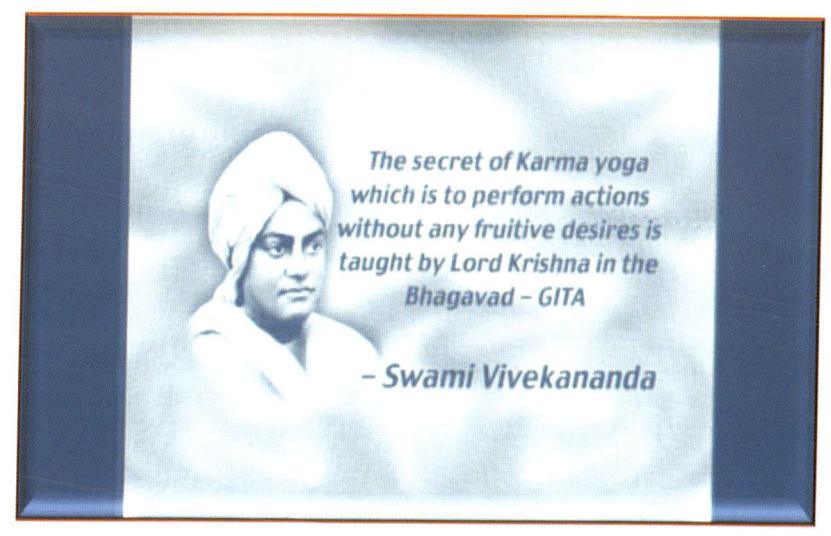

The secret of Karma yoga which is to perform actions without any fruitive desires is taught by Lord Krishna in the Bhagavad – GITA

– Swami Vivekananda

STERLING PUBLISHERS (P) LTD.
Regd. Office: A1/256, Safdarjung Enclave, New Delhi-110029.
Cin: U22110DL1964PTC211907
Phone: +91 82877 98380/ +91 120-6251823
e-mail: mail@sterlingpublishers.in
www.sterlingpublishers.in

The Bhagavad-Gita: A Fresh Approach
© 2022, Rajiv Sachdev, Karan Ahuja and Neeraj Gupta
ISBN 978 93 93853 18 9

Edited by
Sanjiv Sarin

All rights are reserved.
No part of this publication may be reproduced, stored in a retrieval system or transmitted, in any form or by any means, mechanical, photocopying, recording or otherwise, without prior written permission of the original publisher.

Printed in India

Printed and Published by Sterling Publishers Pvt. Ltd.,
Plot No. 13, Ecotech-III, Greater Noida - 201306, Uttar Pradesh, India

Dedication: To Parents and Brother-in-Law

Sh. C.P. Sachdev   **Smt. Sushil Sachdev**   **Sh. Rajinder Malhotra**

Mother Saraswati
Goddess of Education and Knowledge

A new and interesting presentation of the Bhagavad-Gita with photographs on selected chapters— a fascinating and rewarding read.

Dr Karan Singh

From the Authors

All of us been exposed to astrology at some point of time. We understand that our Birth Chart has all our life secrets as to what will happen during the course of the journey of this life. This science, called the "Science of Astrology", is very accurate and reveals everything about us. But we also wonder why these things happen to us and how every individual has a different Birth Chart. We face many ups and downs during our life and they are also related to the position of the stars at that time. Two Planetary forces act on us – one at the time of birth and the other that changes constantly with the motions of the stars.

While this science tells us everything, astrology does not reveal why the events happen. There is a "Science behind this Science" which is revealed in the Bhagavad-Gita, where Lord Krishna Himself has revealed the Science that works based on "Our own Karmas (Actions in Life) and our Nature".

Viewing these two together, i.e., Astrological Science and the Science behind it which is the Science of God explains all the secrets of life and guides us on our way to liberation. We do not want to own the Karmas of past lives because we have no knowledge of those Karmas, but the Planetary System created by the Lord executes and works on us according to the Karmas of our past lives. The Supreme is the witness and writes our destiny and life story while the Planetary System of the nine stars has the role of execution and works on us through our lifetime.

Lord Krishna says in the Bhagavad-Gita, "Arjuna, God abides in the heart of all creatures, causing them to revolve according to their Karma by His illusive power (Maya) as though mounted on a machine."

This book is based on the Srimad Bhagavad-Gita revealed by Lord Krishna around 3134 BCE and on the Sri Brahma Samhita written by Lord Brahma (one of the rare books). The Bhagavad-Gita is one of the most-read books in the world.

While the Bhagavad-Gita is revealed by the Supreme, Sri Brahma Samhita reveals many secrets about the Supreme and all existences Below Time and Above Time.

There is no mention of any religion in the Bhagavad-Gita. It is about the journey of the Soul from one embodiment to another. Human birth is the most important embodiment where one decides the future journey of the Soul inside the body. Other embodiments are consequences of actions performed during the Human birth.

This is all about the Karmas, our actions that decide the future migration to one of the three destinations, i.e., Heavenly worlds, Human birth or the Lower births of animals and insects.

Lord Krishna revealed another destination which is Above Time – the Abode of God where nothing changes with Time because it is Above Time. This is what makes the Bhagavad-Gita a completely new message from the Supreme. While this message was hidden in the scriptures, coming from Supreme gave a completely new life to the devotees of the Supreme.

The Bhagavad-Gita remains a secret in a way since we are still trying to interpret the Lord's messages. This has led to many creative interpretations of the Bhagavad-Gita. Every interpreter interprets it from his or her angle, the state of their spiritual journey and the resulting understanding.

We all represent a dot on a big board that has four outlets. With every action, significant or not, we perform some journey to one of these gates. These gates take us to Heavenly worlds or Human birth or Animal life post completion of the journey in this covering. The fourth gate is the gate that takes an individual Soul Above Time to God's Abode.

The Bhagavad-Gita reveals itself depending on our position or closeness to one of these gates. It guides us towards the righteous path to continue the journey towards God's Abode. As we progress on the journey, it keeps revealing the path to cover the further distance towards God's Abode. This is the reason that it always remains fresh and this has led to many interpretations of the Bhagavad-Gita, as everyone interprets it as per position of their dot and distance from God.

Guru Nanak ji said, "Karmi aapo aapni, key neere key door," i.e., depending on the actions performed by individuals, some are drawn closer to God and some are taken away from God. Guru Nanak ji said "Ek Onkar" which also means only one "OM" and is the un-manifest form. Guru Nanak ji said "Sat Naam" meaning "Ek Onkar" is the only Truth and all pervading.

These messages resonate with messages in Bhagavad-Gita also where "OM, TAT and SAT" has been declared as the triple appellation of Brahma, who is Truth, Consiousness and Bliss.

The scriptures talk of 8.4 million types of births. Out of these 8.4 million, 400,000 are Human births – some are highly blessed and enlightened, performing their duties selflessly and some are engaged in criminal activities day and night. All are performing their journey to one of the destinations.

The Supreme is present all around us in an un-manifest form – watching us, listening to us, guiding us, hearing us. God is present inside everyone as a True-guide and a witness. That is why whatever we do, there is a consciousness that guides us what is the right thing to do – that is Lord Krishna's fragment inside everyone. We must have complete knowledge of how the Supreme is present in us and around us, always guiding for our welfare. At the same time, God is also witness to all our Karmas and that is what becomes the destiny for the future births.

Lord Krishna says in the Bhagavad-Gita, "This knowledge (of both Nirguna and Saguna aspects of Divinity) is a sovereign science, a sovereign secret, supremely holy, most excellent, directly enjoyable, attended with virtue, very easy to practise and imperishable" – Bhagavad-Gita verse 9.2. Dara Shikoh, son of Emperor Shah Jahan, translated the Bhagavad-Gita into Persian language.

The Bhagavad-Gita answers all the questions that come to our mind – where is God? How does God look like? What happens after death and why? What can we change and how? How does God know about everything we think and do? What leads to heaven? Where does God live? What is the difference between Deities and Gods? Why are some people blessed and gifted naturally at birth and some are not? What are His manifested and un-manifested forms? What do we mean when we say latencies of past Karmas and how do they impact us and what should we do? What is a spiritual journey? And many more questions.

Our special thanks to Saachi Shante, Mrs Ronica Shante and Mrs Naresh Ahuja for their great contribution in the "Astrology Aspect" of this book.

Thanks to Anu, Vanshika and Ramit for their contributions.

Our best wishes to the readers for understanding all the answers and messages from Lord Krishna, the Supreme God.

Contents

1. Lord Krishna and the Bhagavad-Gita — 1
2. Blessings by Birth — 13
3. Science of the Soul — 19
4. Heaven Is Below Time; God's Home Is Above Time — 29
5. End of Mahabharata Was Decided before the Battle Began — 35
6. Karmas Decide the Journey of the Soul: One Birth to the Next, to the Next . . . — 39
7. Sacrifice and Spiritual Journey — 47
8. Material Desires: Eternal Enemy of the Wise — 53
9. Devotees Look for God, God Looks for Devotees — 57
10. Failure of Aspirant Yogi Is Success — 69
11. Manifest God and Un-manifest God — 75
12. Yogamaya: The Spiritual Potency of the Supreme — 93
13. Un-manifest God: Brahma – Infinite Consciousness — 99
14. Cosmic Day and Cosmic Night — 113
15. Three Gunas: Three Destinations — 117
16. Lord Narayana: The Primeval Being — 125
17. Bhagavad-Gita: An Astrological Aspect — 129
18. Key Verses in Bhagavad-Gita with Deep Messages — 147

Bhagavad-Gita Changes Latencies of Past Karmas

If one reads Bhagavad-Gita very sincerely and with all seriousness, then by the grace of the Lord the reactions of his past misdeeds will not act upon him.
– Lord Shiva to Mother Parvati – *Gita Mahatmaya*

CHAPTER 1
Lord Krishna and the Bhagavad-Gita

Lord Krishna

The Supreme Lord Govinda manifests on Planet Earth as Krishna and revealed the secret of life in the Bhagavad-Gita – the secret that had gone missing from the earth and cannot be found in the Vedas, the oldest scriptures.

Lord Krishna, who appeared on earth, was the complete incarnation of the Supreme or we can say the Supreme came on Earth.

Only in this incarnation, did the Lord start eradicating sins and start killing demons from the age of two days. He had killed most of the demons before He was five years old. Everything was performed in such a playful manner that no one realized who He was until He revealed His identity to His devotee Arjuna in the battle of Mahabharata when He was possibly around 80 years old.

The Lord did not fight during the battle. He did not use any arms. In this incarnation the Lord wanted to establish the "Role of Karmas – Actions in Life". This battle also proved that the Lord is with the "Right" and the "Right" will always win.

This also established that there is an unseen form of God all around us that is coaching, guiding and also monitoring us all the time to decide our future births. The Lord is inside us and all around us.

The Lord established that the Supreme is a Friend, Father, Guide and Husband and not someone whom people should fear. The Supreme drove the chariot of His devotee during the battle.

Negative forces had become so powerful that without Lord Krishna's appearance, Righteousness would have lost its foundation on Planet Earth.

Vedas and Bhagavad-Gita

A Brahmana who has obtained enlightenment has as much use for all the Vedas as one who stands at the brink of a sheet of water overflowing on all sides, has for a small reservoir of water – Lord Krishna – Bhagavad-Gita 2.46.

Vedas are our ancient scriptures that have been with us from the time of creation of this earth. Vedas have answers to all our problems – kings who need victory, parents who need children, power, money, overcoming enemies, medicines and solutions to Human defects – name it and there is a mantra or fasting or yajna that can fulfil all our desires. However, anything that we desire and obtain in this material world is with us only till the end of this birth. Death snatches everything away in a split second. Birth gives riches or sufferings depending on where we are reborn. All our Karmas and Desires at the end of this life lead us to the Heavenly Abode or another Human birth or Lower births of Animals and Insects.

God's Abode is Above Time where nothing changes with Time and which is above all these material pleasures and material sufferings. An enlightened person is not attached to these material desires because he or she realizes the truth about the Lord and the Lord's Abode which is Above Time.

Enlightened persons see God all around; enlightened persons see God in everyone; enlightened persons see God's blessings everywhere. This realization enlightens them; this enlightenment lifts them above the material desires and the so-called happiness from these material desires.

Lord Krishna tells Arjuna that an enlightened person values God's Realization much above the means to attain material happiness. God is overflowing with blessings all around, all the time. Vedas are a set of means or a limited reservoir which have also emerged from God but realizing God's presence has no comparison to the set of rules for attainment of temporary happiness.

Enlightenment is a state when a person has sufficiently advanced on the Spiritual Journey and has risen above the Material Journey. Life is a journey – direction matters. An enlightened person loves God.

Reactions of Karmas Never End

God abides in the heart of all creatures, causing them to revolve according to their Karma by His illusive power (Maya) as though mounted on a machine – Lord Krishna – BG 18.61.

We are all mounted on a machine that is set in motion by God but controlled by our Karmas. You see small children sitting on a merry-go-round with a steering in hand. While the child feels that child is driving, it is the underlying machine that is driving. The same is our status and we will not be able to overrule the system if our past Karmas do not support us – time check on our Karmas.

Battle of Mahabharata: The Setting of Bhagavad-Gita

The Mahabharata was a historical battle that was fought on the grounds of Kurukshetra more than 5,000 years ago. When the war was about to begin, disciple and key warrior Arjuna decided not to fight as he saw no good in the battle. That was the time when Lord Krishna stopped Time and revealed the Bhagavad-Gita to Arjuna. Time stopped means that Lord Krishna and Arjuna were talking in the battlefield, and the rest of everything became still. No other incarnation has stopped Time. But Lord Krishna did it few times during His presence on this earth. Time stopped completely and stopped the Planetary System.

Now let us also try to understand who the audience was, i.e., Arjuna. He was in no way an ordinary Human Being – that we know by the simple means that his chariot was driven by Lord Krishna Himself, so his devotion to the Lord was unmatched. He was a Gudakesh, which means he had won over sleep; he did not sleep for 18 days during the time the Mahabharata was fought. He could ascend to the Heavenly Abode with the same body. He was a Maharathi, which means he could fight with 10,000 bowmen alone and he was Savyasachin, which means he could shoot arrows with his left hand as skillfully as with his right hand. He was the son of Indra, the King of Heaven.

Battle of Mahabharata: The Setting of Bhagavad-Gita

Lord Krishna gave two reasons to Arjuna to fight the battle:

"This is an unsolicited war" – Lord Krishna to Arjuna in Bhagavad-Gita verse 2.32. This battle was forced on the Pandavas after every effort to settle peacefully with the opposite forces of Kauravas had failed.

The second reason Lord Krishna gave to Arjuna was, ***"You grieve over those who should not be grieved for" – Bhagavad-Gita verse 2.11.*** Lord Krishna said that while those on the opposite side were relatives, they had indulged in wrong doings and the time had come to free them from their current bodies. Some of them were pious and knew well about Lord Krishna but they were bound to the opposite forces. Lord Krishna said that even the pious person attached to wrong had to leave their bodies. The pious people supporting the wrong were bound because of their vachna (vows) and knew that they would get defeated because the Lord was present on the other side. But they could not undo their vows and looked forward to their deaths to get free from the bodies that were supporting the wrong. This was another message from Lord Krishna – that no one should take a vow because you do not know what complications can come up with time because of the vow. The Lord even advised those on the opposite side to forget their vows that had put them on the wrong path without their wish. But this was something that they did not want to do and they chose to stay with their vows and get killed in the battle. Because of their piousness, they know Lord Krishna was Supreme God and they looked forward to their own deaths.

Knowledge That Had Gone Missing from the Earth Was Revealed by the Lord

- *I revealed this immortal Yoga to Vivasvan (Sun-god); Vivasvan conveyed it to (his son) Manu; and Manu imparted it to (his son) Iksvaku. Thus, transmitted in succession from father to son, Arjuna, this Yoga remained known to Rajarsis (royal sages). Through long lapse of time, this Yoga got lost to the world. The same ancient Yoga, which is the supreme secret, has this day been imparted to you by Me, because you are My devotee and friend – Lord Krishna – BG 4.1.3.*

- *Those who, by practising this knowledge, have entered into My being, are not born again at the Cosmic Dawn, nor feel disturbed even during the Cosmic Dissolution (Pralaya) – Lord Krishna – BG 14.2.*

Lord Krishna has stated that the Knowledge that He has imparted to Arjuna had gone missing from the earth. He had revealed this knowledge to the Sun-god, but with over time, it disappeared from the earth. So we can understand that this knowledge cannot be found in other scriptures.

Also, Lord Krishna stated, those who have practised this knowledge have gone to My Abode which is Above Time. All universes and Heavenly Abodes are Below Time. At the time of the Cosmic Dawn, all these universes are created by Lord Brahma and at the time of Cosmic Night, all universes are dissolved. At the time of Cosmic Night, all Souls who have not crossed the Timeline merge into Brahma and at the time of Cosmic Dawn, they are again born according to their Karmas. Karmas never leave the Soul even when the universes are dissolved. The Bhagavad-Gita has the promise of taking us Above Time. Such a knowledge is revealed by the Supreme Himself.

Lord Krishna as Seen by Lord Brahma, the Creator of the Universe

Krishna, who is also known as Govinda, is the Supreme Godhead. He has an eternal blissful body. He is the origin of all. He has no other origin, and He is the prime cause of all causes.

– Lord Brahma (Creator of the Universe) in Sri Brahma Samhita

Lord Chaitanya Mahaprabhu appeared on Planet Earth in 14th century. He is worshipped as an incarnation of Lord Krishna with moods of Mother Radha. Lord Krishna saw Radha always happy because she was always chanting Krishna's name and Lord Krishna wanted to get the same taste. Chaitanya Mahaprabhu went to Adi Keshav temple in South India and asked for the 5th chapter of Brahma Samhita. This chapter has all the secrets about the appearance of Lord Krishna. When Lord Brahma had the vision of Above Time, He saw Krishna as the origin of All and Krishna has no other origin. Brahma Samhita, a small book, has beautiful explanations of the worlds Below Time and Above Time. This book is written by Lord Brahma, the Creator of the Universe.

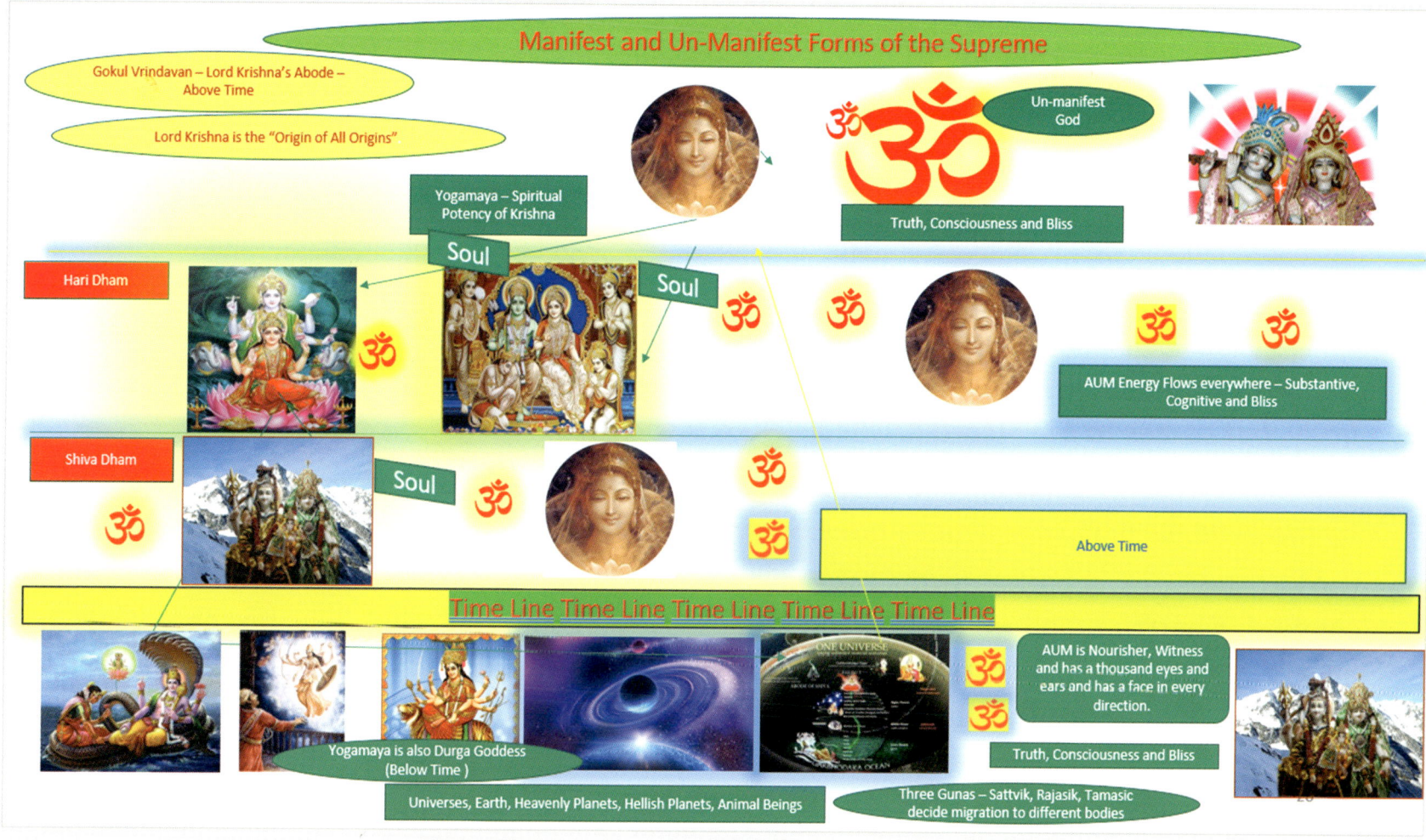

The Supreme Manifests on Earth in Human Form 5,200 Years Ago

Neither gods nor great sages know the secret of My birth – I am the prime cause of gods and great seers– Lord Krishna – BG 10.2.

- *Whenever righteousness is on the decline, unrighteousness is in the ascendant, then I body Myself forth – Lord Krishna – BG 4.7.*
- *For the protection of the virtuous, for the extirpation of evil-doers, and for establishing Dharma (righteousness) on a firm footing, I manifest Myself from age to age – Lord Krishna – BG 4.8.*
- *My birth and activities are divine. He who knows this in reality is not reborn on leaving his body, but comes to Me – Lord Krishna – BG 4.9.*
- *Completely rid of attachment, fear and anger, wholly absorbed in Me, depending on Me, and purified by the penance of wisdom, many have become one with Me in the past – Lord Krishna – BG 4.10.*

> Lord Krishna or His partial forms take incarnations from time to time with the purpose to re-establish Dharma on a firm footing and to destroy the evil-doers. God does not eliminate them because the Universes are run on the Theory of Karmas and hence every incarnation re-enforces the message of performing the Right Karmas.

> Lord Krishna was not an incarnation but Supreme Himself who appeared on earth. Since the Lord is above all gods, His incarnation was not known to even Gods.

> Since the Supreme appeared Himself, He showed the path to His Abode of Hari Dham and Golok Dham where the Lord resides, and which is Above Time and Above all miseries. The Lord revealed that many have become one with Him in the past – ones who followed Him and depended on Him.

Follow the Scriptures (Not Own Sweet Will) for Spiritual Advancement

- *Discarding the injunctions of the scriptures, he who acts in an arbitrary way according to his own sweet will, such a person neither attains occult powers, nor the supreme goal, nor even happiness – Lord Krishna – BG 16.23.*

- *Therefore, the scriptures alone are your guide in determining what should be done and what should not be done. Knowing this, you ought to perform only such action as is ordained by the scriptures – Lord Krishna – BG 16.24.*

As Humans, we always tend to follow our own instincts and intelligence as per our Nature. Hence definitions of what is right and what is wrong varies from one person to another. Chapter 17 of the Bhagavad-Gita explains in detail about this. **"Untutored Innate Faith" – Bhagavad-Gita 17.2** that varies from one to another as per our Nature. Arjuna, as we saw, was a highly spiritual and Lord Krishna questioned his source of knowledge. When such an elevated person close to God needed the knowledge of the Bhagavad-Gita, we can imagine how much this knowledge means to us.

Untutored Faith: Our Mental Disposition

- *People who practise severe penance of an arbitrary type, not sanctioned by the scriptures, and who are full of hypocrisy and egotism and are obsessed with desire, attachment and pride of power. And those who emaciate the elements constituting their body as well as Me, the Supreme Spirit, dwelling in their heart – know these senseless people to have a demoniac disposition – Lord Krishna – BG 17.5–17.6.*

- *An oblation which is offered, a gift given, an austerity practised and whatever good deed is performed, if it is without faith, it is termed as naught, i.e., asat; therefore, it is of no avail here or hereafter – Lord Krishna – BG 17.2.*

Some people observe severe penances of an assumed type. This has been common with Asuras. Such severe penances, if not as per scriptures, are not accepted by Lord Krishna. The Lord's fragment is in the heart of every creature and severe penances hurt the Souls sitting inside. These people are strong in their arbitrary desires. They should abandon them.

Also, if we participate in auspicious acts without faith, these acts do no good to us in this birth or after death. Faith makes a Human Being. Faith defines the Human Being.

CHAPTER 2
Blessings by Birth

Blessings by Birth

There are 400,000 types of Human births:
- Some are born with divine properties
- Some are born with demoniac propensities
- Some are born in enlightened families
- Some are born in rich and pious families
- Some are born in environments with conflicts

Our birth in a family or in an environment is not incidental or accidental. There is a perfect science behind that. Our Karmas and Nature decide our birth. There are 8.4 millions types of births. The Nature of all animals and insects is similar, their food habits are all the same. In Humans, we have 0.4 million types. It is not easy to get a Human birth. With a good spiritual discipline, we can reach God's Abode. With average Karmas, we can stay in Human birth but within Human births themselves, there are 400,000 types of births. And with bad Karmas, we can be migrated down to animal births for a defined period. In this short life of ours, Karmas are so important.

The nine stars in our Planetary System have our bio-data and drive the latencies of past Karmas. But as Humans, we have a way to defeat them by performing good Karmas, following the scriptures and then we can go back to God's Home. Astrology is a perfect science and by an accurate study of our Birth Chart, masters of astrology can tell us the major incidents of our life. These are nothing but latencies of past Karmas that can be studied with the position of nine stars at the time of our birth. These nine stars are tasked to give us good or hard times. But as Lord Shiva tells Mother Parvati, with a sincere study of the Bhagavad-Gita, we can defeat the results of misdeeds of past Karmas. Only God's blessings obtained with the performance of good Karmas can defeat our bad destinies within this birth.

Divine or Demoniac Propensities by Birth

Lord Krishna tells Arjuna: You are born with divine propensities – Lord Krishna – BG 16.5.

- The Soul carries Subtle Body (Mind, Intelligence and Ego) from the Physical Body and acquires a new body. Riding on the Soul are our Karmas and Nature. These decide the next birth – Heavenly Planets or Hellish Births or Human Births (400,000 types of Human Births).

- Only in Human Births can we perform new Karmas and decide the next birth and destination. Animal births are punishment for a defined period. Heavenly Planets are for fulfilment of unfulfilled desires during Human birth in return for the meritorious work performed during Human Birth for a defined period. No new Karmas are performed in Heavenly or Hellish Planets.

- Enlightened people see Heaven as a waste of time as it is trading for meritorious Karmas and pauses the Spiritual Journey.

There are only two types of persons in this world, Arjuna, the one possessing a divine Nature and the other possessing a demoniac disposition by birth – Lord Krishna – BG 16.3–16.4, 16.6.

Blessings by Birth

Destiny of Imperfect Yogi with Desires
First Heavenly Domains
Then Birth in Rich and Pious Families

- Even such a person who has strayed from Yoga, obtains the higher worlds (Heaven) to which persons of meritorious deeds alone are entitled, and having resided there for innumerable years, takes birth of pious and prosperous parents – Lord Krishna – BG 6.41.

- He who takes birth in a rich family, though under the sway of his senses, feels drawn towards God by force of the habit acquired in his previous birth; nay, even the seeker of Yoga (in the form of even-mindedness) transcends the fruit of actions performed with some interested motive as laid down in the Vedas – Lord Krishna – BG 6.44.

Destiny of Imperfect Yogi with Dispassion
Birth in Enlightened Families: Rare Birth
(Defeats Journey to Heaven)

- If he is possessed of dispassion, then not attaining to those regions (Heaven) he is born in the family of enlightened Yogis but such a birth in this world is very difficult to obtain – Lord Krishna – BG 6.42.

- He automatically regains in that birth the latencies of even-mindedness of his previous birth; and through that he strives harder than ever for perfection in the form of God-realization – Lord Krishna – BG 6.43.

Blessings by Birth

- Lord Krishna explained the Journey of an Imperfect Yogi to Arjuna. The Yogi who started walking on the spiritual path but does not succeed completely in this birth does not fall down but rather continues his journey from the next birth.

Two clear destinies of an Imperfect Yogi:

- One who has unfulfilled desires goes to Heaven, fulfils his desires and then returns to Earth. He is born in the family of prosperous and pious parents. The environment is suitable for him to continue his spiritual journey. The environment matters. He has already fulfilled his desires and is drawn towards God. He basically starts the journey from where he left.

- The one who had no desires and is in dispassion does not go to Heaven because Heaven is for fulfilling desires. He defeats the journey to Heaven and is born in the family of enlightened Yogis. This is just right for him to make it to God's Abode in that birth. Such a birth is rare.

Such are the blessings by birth for pious people.

Lord Ram, Laxman, Sita, Hanuman

CHAPTER 3

Science of the Soul

Knowledge of the Soul

- Individual Soul is the Personal Identity from birth to birth.
- Individual Soul is a fragment of the Supreme and the presence of Complete God in us.
- Individual Soul is the Witness, True Guide, Selfless Friend.
- Soul is Un-manifest, Eternal, Imperishable, Immutable.

❖ **The spirit dwelling in this body is really the same as the Supreme. He has been spoken of as the Witness, the True Guide, the Sustainer of All, the Experiencer (as the embodied Soul), the Overlord and the Absolute as well – Lord Krishna – BG 13.22.**

❖ **As the one Sun illumines the entire universe, so the one Atma (Spirit) illumines the whole body – Lord Krishna – BG 13.33.**

The Soul inside our body is the complete presence of God in us. This Soul, being the complete God, is the witness to all our Karmas. This Soul, being the complete God, is always guiding us on the righteous path. This Soul is a fragment of the Oversoul. This Soul is the presence of Krishna in us.

Knowledge of the Soul: Complete Presence of God in Us

The Soul is a fragment of God in everyone. This is personal. The Soul never dies.

- *The Soul is never born, nor does it ever die; nor having once been, does it ever cease to be, for it is unborn, eternal, everlasting and primeval; even though the body is slain, the Soul is not – Lord Krishna – BG 2.20.*

- *The Soul is eternal, all-pervading, immovable, constant and everlasting – Lord Krishna – BG 2.24.*

- *Hardly any great Soul perceives this Soul as marvellous, scarce another great Soul likewise speaks thereof as marvellous, and scarce another worthy one hears of it as marvellous – Lord Krishna – BG 2.29.*

- Lord Krishna says that not everyone thinks about the Soul, i.e., fragment of God in us that keeps us revolving from one birth to the next depending on our Nature and Karmas. It is only some rare set of people who realize the presence of Soul in them and some rare people explain about it, but only deserving people hear about it. People who are deserving are the ones who have embarked the spiritual journey forward by adopting righteous Karmas and by purifying their Nature.

- All material things including our bodies are made of five elements – Fire, Water, Air, Ether and Earth. Every living and non-living thing is made of these elements. But the Soul is not. That is why the Soul can survive even if it were to pierce through the Sun. The Soul is a fragment of the Supreme Lord and belongs to God's Abode – Above Time.

- When will this Soul realize the real Home and start the journey towards it is what Lord Krishna revealed in the Bhagavad-Gita.

Soul: Un-manifest and No Relationship with the Five Tatvas

- *Weapons cannot cut it nor can fire burn it; water cannot wet it nor can wind dry it – Lord Krishna – BG 2.23.*
- *This Soul is un-manifest; it is incomprehensible, and it is spoken of as immutable – Lord Krishna – BG 2.25.*
- *This Soul dwelling in the bodies of all; it can never be slain – Lord Krishna – BG 2.30.*
- *As the all-pervading ether is not contaminated by reason of its subtlety, though permeating the body, the Self is not affected by the attributes of the body due to its attribute-less character – Lord Krishna – BG 13.32.*

Lord Krishna explains the Soul that is present in every one of us. It is un-manifest, which means it will never appear in a form. The Soul will always be invisible. It cannot be stopped or muted. Even when all the universes are destroyed, the Soul will always pass through any disaster. Also, the Soul present in everyone of us will stay same, i.e., pure like God because it is a fragment of God. Even if the body performs foul Karmas, it does not impact the Soul. While bad Karmas will lead to bad embodiments, i.e., birth as animals or in Hellish Worlds, Soul will still remain pure. This is because of the attribute-less character of the Soul.

Soul's Relationship with the Supreme: Witness, Guide

- *The Spirit or Soul dwelling in this body is really the same as the Supreme. It has also been spoken of as the Witness, the True Guide, the Sustainer of all, the Experiencer (as the embodied Soul), the Overlord and the Absolute – Lord Krishna – BG 13.22.*

- *He alone truly sees, who sees the Supreme Lord as imperishable and abiding equally in all perishable beings, both animate and inanimate – Lord Krishna – BG 13.27.*

- *Prakriti is said to be responsible for bringing forth the evolutes and the instruments, while the individual Soul is declared to be responsible for the experience of joys and sorrows – Lord Krishna – BG 13.20.*

When our Nature and Karmas are not pure, the Soul inside our body, despite being pure (because the Soul is complete God) ends up experiencing the sufferings that it has to go through as determined by God's system. We have to watch Karmas that get influenced by our Nature as Karmas in Human birth can take us to God's Home Above Time or Heavenly Planets or Human births. There are 400,000 types of Human births or Hellish births in insects and animals. Our short life of a few decades can end in great blessings or a big disaster – the choice is ours as we perform Karmas.

Soul Is Imperishable and Keeps Us Alive in the Body

- ❖ *As the one Sun illumines this entire universe, so the one Atma (Spirit) illumines the whole Ksetra (Field) – Lord Krishna – BG 13.33.*

- ❖ *The eternal Jivatma in this body is a fragment of My own Self; and it is that alone which draws around itself the mind and the five senses, which abide in Prakriti – Lord Krishna – BG 15.7.*

- ❖ *Jivatma or the embodied Soul is imperishable – Lord Krishna – BG 15.16.*

- ➤ We are alive because of the Soul inside. We breathe because of the Soul inside. Our system works because of the Soul. Our Consciousness is because of the Soul. Our thinking works because of the Soul. We will be just a body in the absence of the Soul. Death means the Soul is gone out from the body to the next destination as per our Nature and Karmas.

- ➤ Lord Krishna clearly says that this Soul or Jivatma is My Fragment so we have God sitting inside us – it is a matter of realization. Realization will come with purity of Mind and Karmas. Lord Krishna says that this Soul is imperishable and will always be alive – we cannot imagine any existence without God, and Soul is the same as God.

Individual Soul Is Consciousness but Does Not Perform Karmas

❖ *Indestructible supreme Spirit, though dwelling in the body, in fact does nothing, nor gets tainted – Lord Krishna – BG 13.31.*

❖ *Whose heart has not been purified, know not this Self in spite of their best endeavours – Lord Krishna – BG 15.11.*

➢ The Soul inside us is a True Guide, Frie nd and Witness because the Soul is God inside us with a Personal Identity that we carry from one birth to the next to the next. The Soul does not perform Karmas.

➢ The Soul is Live God inside us keeping us alive, guiding us on the righteousness path, guiding us where we belong – God's Abode Above Time. Our good or bad Karmas do not make any changes to the Soul.

➢ The Karmas change our coverings, i.e., birth in enlightened family or rich and pious family or struggling environment in the Human birth and lead us to Heavenly Planets or Hellish Births.

➢ To realize the presence of God in us, we must purify our hearts, else all attempts will fail.

Soul Migration: One Body to the Next, Based on Nature and Karmas

- ❖ *It is the attachment with three Gunas that is responsible for the birth of this Soul in good or evil wombs – Lord Krishna – BG 13.21.*
- ❖ *Even as the wind wafts scents from their seat, so too the Jivatma, which is the controller of the body etc., taking the mind and the senses from the body which it leaves behind, forthwith migrates to the body which it acquires – Lord Krishna – BG 15.8.*
- ❖ *It is while dwelling in the senses of hearing, sight, touch, taste and smell, as well as in the mind, that this Jivatma enjoys the objects of senses – Lord Krishna – BG 15.9.*
- ❖ *Desire, anger and greed – these triple gates of hell, bring about the downfall of the Soul – Lord Krishna – BG 16.21.*

- ➤ Sattivik (Mode of Goodness), Rajasik (Mode of Inertia) and Tamasic (Mode of Ignorance).

- ➤ Sattivik is noble and enlightening, Rajasik is Actions with Greed and Desires, Tamasic is bad actions not recommended by the scriptures.

- ➤ Attachment to these Gunas leads to Higher and Lower births. When the Soul leaves our body, the Soul takes the Mind, Senses and Karmas along. A person who dies as an angry person will be born as an angry person. Sum of Nature and Karmas decide the type of next birth.

- ➤ Material desires, anger and greed spoil our Nature and Karmas and hence spoil the spiritual journey. God's system is a witness of all our deeds and decides our next birth.

Adhyatama: Soul Remains a Personal Identity from One Birth to the Next

- *One's own Self (the individual Soul) is called Adhyatama – Lord Krishna – BG 8.3.*

- *Before birth, beings are not manifest to our Human senses; on death they return to the Un-manifest again. They are manifest only in the interim between birth and death – Lord Krishna – BG 2.28.*

- *In fact, there was never a time when I was not, or when you or these kings were not. Nor is it a fact that hereafter we shall all cease to be – Lord Krishna – BG 2.12.*

- *Just as boyhood, youth and old age are attributed to the Soul through this body, even so it attains another body – Lord Krishna – BG 2.13.*

- *As a man shedding worn-out garments takes other new ones, likewise, the embodied Soul, casting off worn-out bodies, enters into others that are new – Lord Krishna – BG 2.22.*

Lord Krishna says that the Soul inside us has a personal identity and it carries our personal identity from birth to birth. The Soul is un-manifest before it enters this body, it cannot be seen and after it exits this body, it can not be seen either. But the Soul never dies; the Soul just changes the covering depending on our Karmas. The new body is just another stage like childhood to youth and youth to old age. While we can relate the change from childhood to youth and old age as this happens in the same body, we are unable to realize the change when the Soul changes the body. It is just that after a time, the Soul has to exit the body because the body gets worn out. The Soul carries all the performances of this birth and decides on the body to take in the next birth.

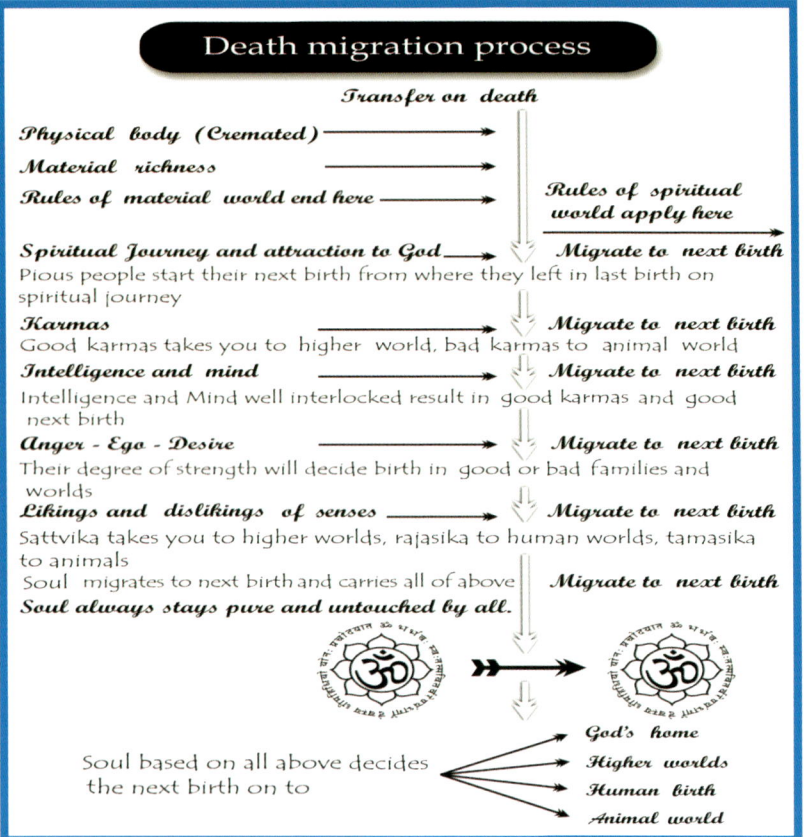

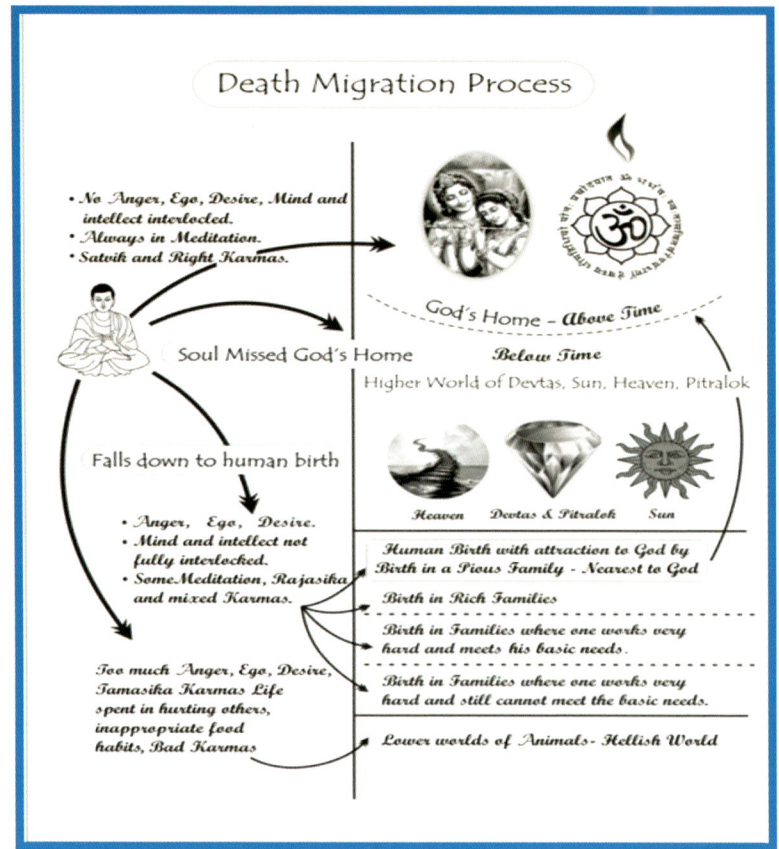

शरीरं यदवाप्नोति यच्चाप्युत्क्रामतीश्वर: |
गृहीत्वैतानि संयाति वायुर्गन्धानिवाशयात् ||

Even as the wind wafts scents from their seat, so, too, the Jivatama, which is the controller of the body etc., taking the mind and the senses from the body which it leaves behind, forthwith migrates to the body which it acquires – Lord Krishna – BG 15.8.

CHAPTER 4

Heaven Is Below Time;
God's Home Is Above Time

Heaven Is Below Time; God's Home Is Above Time

- Lord Brahma's (Creator of the universe) abode is also Below Time.
- Heavenly Planets are Below Time.
- Only God's Abode is Above Time.
- There are many, many universes that exist in parallel.

Heaven Is Not on the Way to God's Home

Material Desires Keep the Intellect Away from God

- *Those who are full of worldly desires and devoted to the letter of the Vedas, who look upon Heaven as the supreme goal and argue that there is nothing beyond Heaven, are unwise. They utter flowery speech recommending many rituals of various kinds for the attainment of pleasure and power with rebirth as their fruit. Those whose minds are carried away by such words and who are deeply attached to pleasures and worldly power, cannot attain the determinate intellect concentrated on God – Lord Krishna – BG 2.42–2.44.*

- *A Brahmana who has obtained enlightenment, has as much use for all the Vedas as one who stands at the brink of a sheet of water overflowing on all sides has for a small reservoir of water – Lord Krishna – BG 2.46.*

➤ The Vedas, our ancient scriptures, have answers to every problem. If we need power or wealth or want to fulfil any wish, there are mantras. But Lord Krishna cautions that those who are attached to the worldly material pleasures and follow the scriptures to fulfil their wishes do not have the wisdom of attaining God. They are after fulfilment of their wishes and know that the scriptures have the means to attain the worldly pleasures. These people, with the best of Karmas but with desires, can at most reach Heavenly Planets but cannot come out of the cycles of birth-and-death.

➤ However, an enlightened person who realizes that all this material happiness is temporary, falls in love with God. He does not use God to fulfil his desires but loves God and does not have material desires. He is an enlightened person. Since he does not have material desires, he does not need the scriptures that have answers about getting the desires fulfilled. An enlightened person sees God everywhere. He has admiration and love is for the Supreme and does not wish for petty and perishable objects. Hence, he is like a person standing on the brink of a sheet of water, overflowing on all sides, whereas the Vedas are like a small reservoir in comparison, that merely provide mantras for fulfilment of worldly desires. The enlightened person is a God-loving Soul.

God's Home Is Above Time: Even Brahmaloka Is Below Time

Heavens, Universes and Hellish Planets Are All Below Time

All the worlds from Brahmaloka (the heavenly realm of the Creator Brahma) downwards are liable to birth and rebirth. But O son of Kunti, on attaining Me, there is no re-birth (For, while I am beyond Time, regions like Brahmaloka, being conditioned by Time, are transitory) – Lord Krishna – BG 8.16.

Above Time: No rebirth, No impact of Time

Below Time: Brahmaloka, Heavenly Planets, Universes and Hellish Planets

Reality about Time

Brahma's day covers a thousand Mahayugas, and Brahma's night extends to another thousand Mahayugas – Lord Krishna – BG 8.17.

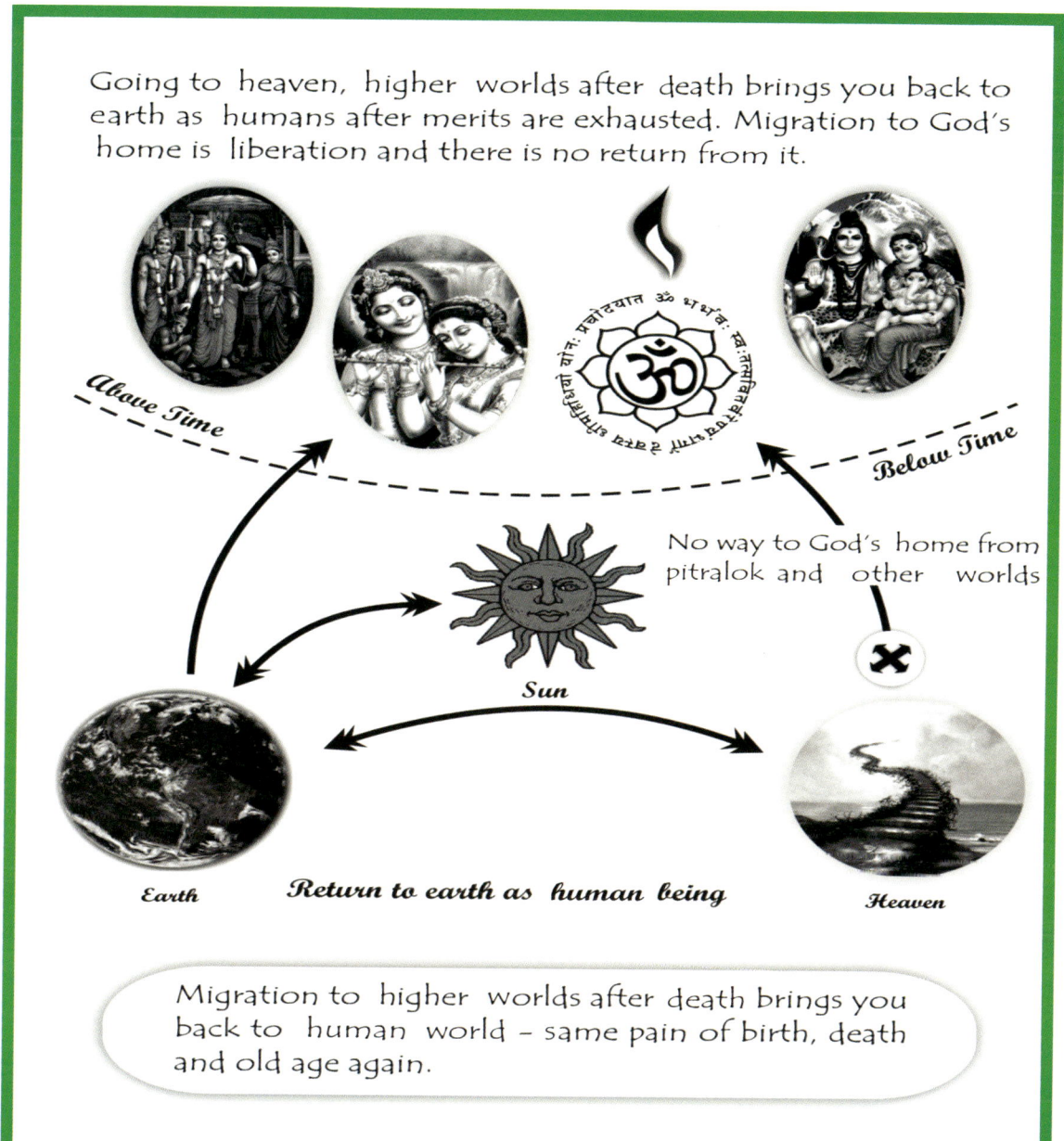

Lord Shiva, Parvati, Ganesha

CHAPTER 5

End of Mahabharata Was Decided before the Battle Began

End of Mahabharata Was Decided by the Lord before the Battle Began: Theory of Karma

Lord Krishna showed to Arjuna His divine forms and showed all universes, Gods and Deities within Him.

Lord Krishna said to Arjuna, I am the mighty Kala (the eternal Time-spirit), the destroyer of the worlds. I am out to exterminate these people. Even without you all these warriors arrayed in the enemy's camp shall die. These warriors stand already slain by Me; be you only an instrument, Arjuna – Lord Krishna – BG 11.32–11.33.

This is a very important aspect of the Mahabharata and the Bhagavad-Gita. Lord Krishna did not participate in the war but drove the chariot of His devotee Arjuna. Until the Lord revealed His true identity to Arjuna while revealing Bhagavad-Gita, even Arjuna did not know His true identity – that Lord Krishna was the complete Supreme on earth. The Lord showed to Arjuna all the gods, demi-gods and universes within Him. The Bhagavad-Gita was revealed on Day 1 of Mahabharata, before the battle started. Arjuna saw the end of the battle in Lord Krishna's universal form whereas the battle had not even started. Hence Arjuna asked Lord Krishna about His identity and the Lord revealed to Arjuna that He had decided to exterminate these people and hence the end of battle was already decided – Karmas had decided the outcome of the battle.

- यदा यदा हि धर्मस्य ग्लानिर्भवति भारत ।
  अभ्युत्थानमधर्मस्य तदात्मानं सृजाम्यहम् ॥

- *Whenever there is a decline in righteousness and an increase in unrighteousness, O Arjuna, at that time I manifest myself on earth – Lord Krishna – BG 4.7.*

- परित्राणाय साधूनां विनाशाय च दुष्कृताम् ।
  धर्मसंस्थापनार्थाय सम्भवामि युगे युगे ॥

- *To protect the righteous, to annihilate the wicked and to reestablish the principles of dharma, I appear on this earth, age after age – Lord Krishna – BG 4.8.*

End of Mahabharata Was Decided by the Lord before the War Began

Reinforces Theory of Karmas and Results of Karmas under the Supreme

- *These warriors stand already slain by Me; be you only an instrument, Arjuna – Lord Krishna – BG 11.33.*

Krishna had already decided to kill all these warriors and that is what Arjun saw in Virat form of Lord Krishna. Arjuna had been chosen as the instrument for doing this task based on his Nature and Divine Endowments because he was doing a task for the Lord and not for himself. This also proves that God's system is behind the key actions that happen in the universe. These actions are based on individual karmas which becomes very clear in Chapter 18 during the concluding messages from the Lord to Arjuna.

- *Fight and you will surely conquer the enemies in the war – Lord Krishna – BG 11.34.*

Krishna again explains that there is God's force working and Arjuna is bound to win. Krishna had already explained in the previous verse that these warriors will die even if Arjuna does not fight because the decision was taken by God to eradicate these warriors. However, when we study verse 59 to verse 61 of Chapter 18, the Lord explained to Arjuna as how Arjuna will definitely fight this battle because **"God Abides in the heart of all creatures, causing them to revolve according to their Karma by His illusive power (Maya) as though mounted on a machine."**

Mother Durga

CHAPTER 6
Karmas Decide the Journey of the Soul: One Birth to the Next, to the Next . . .

Righteous Karmas (Actions in Life) Are Supreme

कर्मण्येवाधिकारस्ते मा फलेषु कदाचन |
मा कर्मफलहेतुर्भूर्मा ते सङ्गोऽस्त्वकर्मणि ||

Your right is to work only and never to the fruit thereof. Do not consider yourself to be the cause of the fruit of action, nor let your attachment be to inaction – Lord Krishna – BG 2.47.

God has a system of deciding the results. Humans should not further intervene in His system. Results depend on Karmas performed in this life and previous births (latencies of past births), Nature, spiritual journey of the individual Soul and God's blessings. Human intervention is temporary even when it is effective, but this is a futile effort. God's un-manifest form is seeing us with a thousand eyes, a thousand ears and face on all sides. He is all pervading. He is the True Guide, Well-wisher and Witness also. His presence all around is observed by devotees as Aum or OM.

Our Karmas Revolve Us as If We Are Mounted on a Machine

ईश्वरः सर्वभूतानां हृद्देशेऽर्जुन तिष्ठति | भ्रामयन्सर्वभूतानि यन्त्रारूढानि मायया ||

God abides in the hearts of all creatures, causing them to revolve according to their Karmas by His illusive power (Maya) as though mounted on a machine – Lord Krishna – BG 18.61.

We are all mounted on a machine. We think that we are driving our destinies but there is a bigger force, which is Lord's system, that is making us go round and that Lord's system is driving us according to our past Karmas. So the need is to watch our Karmas and surrender all actions to the Lord.

Karmas Decide the Future Journey of the Soul

- *In this world there is no purifier as great as knowledge; he who has attained purity of heart through prolonged practise of Karmayoga automatically sees the light of truth in the Self in course of time – Lord Krishna – BG 4.38.*

- *Poor and wretched are those who are the cause in making their actions bear fruit – Lord Krishna – BG 2.49.*

- *God determines neither the doership nor the doings of men, nor even their contact with the fruit of actions; but it is Nature alone that does all this – Lord Krishna – BG 5.14.*

➢ God's system is working and deciding the fruits for our actions. Our manipulations are short-lived and get the sufferings.

➢ God's presence in our hearts as Jiva and God's presence all around us in the un-manifest form of Brahma or OM decides the fruits and journey of the Soul.

➢ Jiva (Soul): Personal, moves from birth-to-birth depending on Karmas and Nature. This is a fragment of God in everyone, Un-manifest is known as Adhiyajna (Witness and True Guide). This is Lord Krishna.

➢ Brahma or OM : Un-manifest Divinity, Impersonal, Nourisher, Has face on every side, has thousands of eyes, ears, hands and feet and is present all around us. Brahma's Nature is: Truth – Consciousness – Bliss.

➢ God does nothing. We perform everything either through our own decisions influenced by our Nature or under the influence of our past Karmas. Hence we are responsible for the results of every action.

The Karmayogi Who Keeps His Mind Fixed on God Reaches Brahma in No Time

- *The Karmayogi who keeps his mind fixed on God, reaches Brahma in no time – Lord Krishna – BG 5.6.*

- *The Karmayogi, who has fully conquered his mind and mastered his senses, whose heart is pure, and who has identified himself with the Self of all beings (viz., God), remains untainted, even though performing action – Lord Krishna – BG 4.7.*

- *He who acts offering all actions to God, and shaking off attachment, remains untouched by sin, as the lotus leaf by water – Lord Krishna – BG 5.10.*

Lord Krishna reveals that Karma yoga is the most assured and quickest way to reach God – Remember Him all the time and perform all your natural duties with a surrender to Him. Without surrender, Karmas produce good, bad and mixed results. The only way to reach His Abode Above Time is surrender.

Karmas (Actions in Life):
One's Own Self Is Friend and Enemy of Self

- ❖ *He who with firm intellect and free from doubt, rejoices not on obtaining what is pleasant and does not feel perturbed on meeting with the unpleasant, that knower of Brahma lives eternally in identity with Brahma – Lord Krishna – BG 5.20.*

- ❖ *To the contemplative Soul who desires to attain Karmayoga, selfless action is said to be the means; for the same man when he is established in Yoga, absence of all Sankalps (thoughts of the world) is said to be the way to blessedness – Lord Krishna – BG 6.3.*

- ❖ *One's own Self is the friend of the Soul by whom the lower Self (consisting of the mind, senses and body) has been conquered; even so, the very Self of him, who has not conquered his lower Self, behaves antagonistically like an enemy – Lord Krishna – BG 6.6.*

- ➢ The Lord advises rising above material distractions. These are temporary and the feelings of happiness and sadness they produce are unreal. Brahma is real and that is realized as OM and is present everywhere – Below Time and Above Time. When a person does not get distracted with material things, he has oneness with Brahma or OM.

- ➢ Sankalps are vows and wishes to fulfil material desires for which one chooses the path described in scriptures, i.e., mantras. A person on the spiritual journey first abandons the thoughts of selfish gains and then stops invoking any means to fulfil his material desires.

- ➢ Lower Self has all the desires hidden. Knowing well that the body will not go beyond this birth, a spiritually Intelligent person conquers the lower Self and rises above the senses to Soul-realization and embarks on the spiritual journey.

God Is Always Working

- *There is no duty in all the three worlds for Me to perform, nor is there anything worth attaining, unattained by Me; yet I continue to work – Lord Krishna – BG 3.22.*
- *From whom all beings come into being and by whom the whole universe is pervaded, by worshipping Him through the performance of His own natural duties, man attains the highest perfection – Lord Krishna – BG 18.46.*
- *One should not relinquish one's innate duty, even though it has a measure of evil; for all undertakings are beset by some evil, as is the fire covered by smoke – Lord Krishna – BG 18.48.*
- *The Karmayogi, who, depends on Me, attains by My grace the eternal, imperishable state, even though performing all actions – Lord Krishna – BG 18.56.*

- Our Soul is a fragment of the Oversoul, Lord Krishna. The Soul derives its purpose and energy from the Oversoul even when we are not conscious about it. Hence if the Lord does not work, all fragments will also get the inspiration of not working.
- The best worship is to perform all our natural duties and that is what the Bhagavad-Gita is all about. Since we have our own limitations of thoughts and understanding, we should realize ourselves as a part of the Lord and surrender all actions to Him. Then we will not perform any sin and all the results of our deeds will be taken by the Lord; and free from results, we will reach God's Abode.
- Arjuna was a born warrior and he was advised by the Lord to fight the unsolicited war to bring righteousness on the Planet Earth. This was the Supreme's advice. Arjuna knew that this task of the warrior for the righteousness would consume many lives but the Lord advised him towards the conclusion of Bhagavad-Gita that duties can have a measure of evil and a person should still not relinquish his duties when he sees a measure of evil – he must perform all his natural, in-born duties.
- This verse has a very deep message. Lord Krishna is asking Arjuna if he is depending on Him. Karmayoga is selflessly performing all your duties but we should not fail to depend on Him. Many creative interpretations can come from this verse depending on the spiritual status of the individuals trying to describe the verse.

Latencies of Past Karmas: Humans Perform Prescribed or Prohibited Actions

❖ ***Humans perform prescribed or prohibited actions under the influence of latencies of past Karmas – Lord Krishna – BG 18.15.***

If one reads the Bhagavad-Gita very seriously and with all seriousness, then by the grace of the Lord the reactions of his past misdeeds will not act upon the person – ***Lord Shiva to Mother Parvati – Gita Mahatmaya.***

Many actions are performed because of the latencies of past Karmas. Our Karmas go with us from one birth to the next to the next. It is our Nature and Karmas that shape our actions. Sometimes we find that some actions get performed with little or no control from us. These actions could be prescribed or prohibited by the scriptures. These could be the result of latencies of past Karmas. This does not mean that our Nature does not play a role in that. Our Nature has a major role in the performance of our actions. Actions performed because of Nature should not be termed as latencies of past Karmas. But Lord Krishna has said in the Bhagavad-Gita that humans perform prescribed or prohibited actions under the influence of latencies of past Karmas.

Karma Yoga Is Superior to Karma Sanyasa

संन्यास: कर्मयोगश्च नि:श्रेयसकरावुभौ | तयोस्तु कर्मसंन्यासात्कर्मयोगो विशिष्यते ||

The Supreme Lord said: Both the path of Karma sanyās (renunciation of actions) and Karma yoga (working in devotion) lead to the supreme goal. But Karma yoga is superior to Karma sanyās – Lord Krishna – BG 5.2.

Karmas decide the journey of the Soul, one birth to the next to the next to the next . . .

The Yogi is superior to ascetics, superior to those versed in sacred lore, superior to those who perform actions with interested motives – Lord Krishna – BG 6.46.

God is witness to all our Karmas in un-manifest form with a thousand ears and a thousand eyes and a face on every side.

CHAPTER 7
Sacrifice and Spiritual Journey

Sacrifice = Purification = Spiritual Journey

- ❖ *The All-Pervading Infinite is always present in sacrifice.*

- ❖ *Without sacrifice even this world is not happy so how can the next one be happy?*

All Pervading Infinite Is Always Present in Sacrifice

- ❖ *The virtuous who partake of what is left over after sacrifice are absolved of all sins. The sinful ones who cook for the sake of nourishing their bodies alone, partake of sin only – Lord Krishna – BG 3.13.*

- ❖ *The all-pervading Infinite is always present in sacrifice – Lord Krishna – BG 3.14.*

- ❖ *Having in viewa of the maintenance of the world order, one should take to action – Lord Krishna – BG 3.20.*

- ➢ Sacrifice is everything that we perform for the sake of others without any selfish motive. Lord Krishna advised Arjuna that all actions that are performed for the sake of sacrifice do not produce any binding results and if we enjoy the leftover, it is not only a nectar but this way of living absolves us from the past sins.

- ➢ The all-pervading Infinite is Brahma. Lord Krishna says that the work performed in sacrifice is like performing the work for Brahma. Brahma, which is OM is the un-manifest form of the Lord.

- ➢ In the process of performing sacrifices, one should not become an odd person. A king should behave like a king. We should not leave our homes or degenerate our living to a point where we get noticed having an odd behavior. We should perform all our sacrifices and duties without compromising on the maintenance of the world order.

Spirit of Sacrifice: Performing All Your Natural Duties

- *He who does not follow the wheel of creation thus set going in this world i.e., does not perform his duties, leads a sinful and sensual life, he lives in vain – Lord Krishna – BG 3.16.*

- *Go on efficiently doing your duty at all times without (seeking any rewards) attachment. Doing work without attachment man attains the Supreme – Lord Krishna – BG 3.19.*

- *Man is bound by his own action except when it is performed for the sake of sacrifice – Lord Krishna – BG 3.9.*

> Our Actions, if not performed for the sake of sacrifice, produce good, bad or mixed results. Good actions produce heavenly rewards, bad actions give hellish punishments and mixed actions have mixed results. To reach God's Abode, all actions have to be dedicated to the Lord.

> Attachment means desires and with them, the person has already defined the outcome of his actions. Such people, at most, reach Heavenly Planets and keep revolving in the cycles of birth-and-death.

> The Lord is working all the time. We are born with our natural duties. Sacrifice lies in performing all our natural duties. If a person does not perform his natural duties, he is living a sinful life, just for sensual enjoyment and is lost in the spiritual journey.

Without Sacrifice Neither This World Is Happy nor Beyond

- *Yogis who enjoy the nectar that has been left over after the performance of a sacrifice attain the eternal Brahma. To the man who does not offer sacrifice, even this world is not happy; how, then, can the other world be happy? – Lord Krishna – BG 4.31.*

- *He who lacks discrimination, is devoid of faith and is at the same time possessed by doubt, is lost to the spiritual path. For the doubting Soul there is neither this world nor the world beyond, nor even happiness – Lord Krishna – BG 4.40.*

Among Sacrifices, I Am the Sacrifice of Japa

- *Sacrifice, charity and penance – all these are purifiers to the wise men – Lord Krishna – BG 18.5.*

- *Among sacrifices, I am the sacrifice of japa (intonation of sacred chants) – Lord Krishna – BG 10.25.*

There are several types of sacrifices mentioned in Bhagavad-Gita but Lord has chosen chanting of Lord's name as the highest form of sacrifice and has confirmed His personal presence in chanting of His holy name. That is why people chant "Hare Krishna", "Radhey-Radhey" or the Mahamantra:

"Hare Krishna, Hare Krishna, Krishna Krishna, Hare Hare,

Hare Rama, Hare Rama, Rama Rama, Hare Hare."

CHAPTER 8

Material Desires:
Eternal Enemy of the Wise

Material Desires: Eternal Enemy of the Wise

- ❖ *As fire is covered by smoke, mirror by dust and embryo by the amnion, so is knowledge covered by desire – Lord Krishna – BG 3.38.*
- ❖ *The senses, the mind and the intellect are declared to be its seat; covering the knowledge through these, it (desire) deludes the embodied Soul – Lord Krishna – BG 3.40.*
- ❖ *Control your senses, and then kill this evil thing which obstructs Jnana (knowledge of the Absolute or Nirguna Brahma) and Vijnana (knowledge of Sakara Brahma or manifest Divinity) – Lord Krishna – BG 3.41.*
- ❖ *Kill the enemy in the form of desire that is hard to overcome – Lord Krishna – BG 3.43.*

- ➢ *Desires are not an easy enemy. They are an eternal enemy because they keep us winning material pleasures and keep us away from the true destination which is Home Above Time or Param Dham or Golok – Lord Krishna and Hari Dham.*
- ➢ *Desires keep us away from the true knowledge of manifest and un-manifest Supreme.*
- ➢ Desires derail our Soul from moving towards its home which is Above Time.
- ➢ Desires obstruct true knowledge of the manifest and un-manifest Supreme.
- ➢ Desires are seeking fruits for the meritorious work and this keeps one away from the Supreme.

Meditation

- *Living in seclusion all by himself, the Yogi who has controlled his mind and body and is free from desires and void of possessions, should constantly engage his mind in meditation – Lord Krishna – BG 6.10.*

- *Constantly applying his mind to Me, the Yogi with a disciplined mind attains everlasting peace consisting of supreme bliss, which abides in Me – Lord Krishna – BG 6.15.*

- *The Yogi whose mind is perfectly serene, who is sinless, whose passion is subdued, and who is identified with Brahma, the embodiment of Truth, Consciousness and Bliss, to such a Yogi supreme happiness comes as a matter of course – Lord Krishna – BG 6.27.*

- *Shutting out all thoughts of external enjoyments, with the gaze fixed on the space between the eye-brows, having regulated the Prana (outgoing) and Apana (incoming) breaths flowing within the nostrils, he who has brought his senses, mind and intellect under control – such a contemplative Soul intent on liberation and free from desire, fear and anger, is ever liberated – Lord Krishna – BG 5.27–5.28.*

- Lord Krishna reveals the way of meditation to Arjuna, i.e., how to control his wandering mind running after desires and bring it to realize the presence of the Supreme.

- Through meditation we can control our mind that makes us run after various desires. All the desires can never be fulfilled as one desire leads to the next and then the next and so on.

- In the Bhagavad-Gita Lord Krishna asks Arjuna to focus his mind on the Lord and then he can taste the real peace which comes only with Supreme's bliss.

- Peaceful and desireless mind is able to relate itself to the all-pervading, subtler than the subtle, always blessing, un-manifest Supreme. That person's happiness is unmatched and he only can realize that happiness and cannot explain that happiness to the materially attracted people.

Lord Hanuman

CHAPTER 9
Devotees Look for God,
God Looks for Devotees

Devotees Look for God, God Looks for Devotees

ये यथा मां प्रपद्यन्ते तांस्तथैव भजाम्यहम् | मम वर्त्मानुवर्तन्ते मनुष्याः पार्थ सर्वशः ||

Howsoever people seek Me, even so do I respond to them; for all people follow My path in every way – Lord Krishna – BG 4.11.

➢ Story of Meera Bai

➢ Story of Vrinda–Tulsi: Love of Lord Krishna for Devotee

➢ Khirachora Gopinath Temple: God Keeps the Offering Preserved for His Devotee

➢ Pagla Baba Mandir: Lord Krishna Appears in Court as a Witness

➢ Sakshi Gopal Mandir: God Travelled with His Devotee

➢ Nidhi Van (Vrindavan): Radha–Krishna Come Every Night, Even Today

Story of Meera Bai

Story of Meera Bai, Princess, Queen. Born in 1499 CE. Remained immersed in love with Lord Krishna. Wrote hundreds of devotional songs that are sung even today with the same love and devotion. Met Lord Krishna in person because of her extreme love. Merged in Lord Krishna's idol and disappeared from earth in front of everyone in Ranchod temple in Orissa.

Story of Meera Bai

Meera Bai was a princess and later a queen after her marriage. She is a great example of Prema Bhakti. She spent all her life in love for Lord Krishna and sang hundreds of devotional songs in praise of Lord Krishna.

She was born in 1499 in Rajasthan. She was married to Rana Kumbha. Lord Krishna met her a few times during her lifetime.

It is believed that the turning point in Meera's life, which precipitated her departure from Mewar and hence her earthly bonds, occurred when once Akbar, the Mughal King and his court musician Tansen came in disguise to Chittore to hear her devotional and inspiring songs. Both entered the temple and listened to Meera's soul-stirring songs to their heart's content.

Akbar was really moved. Before he departed, he touched the holy feet of Meera and placed a necklace of priceless gems in front of the idol of Lord Krishna as a present. Rana Kumbha was told that Akbar had entered the temple. He asked Meera to leave the palace for which he later repented a lot but could not bring Meera back.

Meera, in all her life, never got angry even though she went through a lot of troubles. She was given poison and she drank it, but nothing happened to her. She was sent a poisonous cobra snake but when she opened the box, it became a garland.

Towards the later years of her life, she went to Vrindavan as she was asked by Lord Krishna to go there. The end of her life came when she danced in front of Lord Krishna's idol in the Ranchod temple in Orissa. She disappeared and it is believed that she entered the idol because the doors of the temple suddenly closed and then her chunni was found wrapped around the feet of Krishna's idol. The people did not find Meera anywhere inside the temple or outside.

Story of Vrinda–Tulsi

Tulsi or Basil is considered so auspicious that:
- Every offering to God has a Tulsi leaf in it as Lord accepts the offering with Tulsi.
- Tulsi and Krishna in His Shaligram form are married in the month of Kartik.
- Lord Krishna's Vrindavan is in the name of Vrinda (Tulsi).
- One leaf of Tulsi was more than the weight of Lord Krishna on a weighing scale – Story of Satyabhama – Love of God for His devotees.
- One leaf of Tulsi satisfied the hunger of Hanuman.

On Kartik Purnima (Full Moon), Lord Krishna Himself worships Tulsi with these eight names:

1. Vrindavani
2. Vrinda
3. Vishvapujita
4. Pushpa-Asara
5. Nandini
6. Krishnajivini
7. Vishva-Pavani
8. Tulsi

Story of Vrinda–Tulsi: Love of Lord Krishna for Devotee

In Hinduism, we worship Tulsi or Tulsa. Tulsi is offered to Lord Krishna. This holy plant has a human face to it – Vrinda. Lord Krishna's Vrindavan is named after Vrinda. The Lord happily accepts offerings accompanied with a Tulsi leaf as it makes the offering pure.

Once Lord Krishna was being weighed on a weighing scale as Satyabhama (Lord's wife) wanted to offer gold equal to Krishna's weight to the priest, Narada ji. All the available gold was not enough to match the weight of the Supreme. Then Mother Rukmini intervened and advised to remove all the gold from the scales and place a leaf of Tulsi instead. Just one leaf of Tulsi lifted pan of the weighing scale on which He was sitting – Lord Krishna, the Supreme, One Who lives Above Time, One Who owns all the universes, One Who has no one equal to Him.

Vrinda worshipped Lord Krishna with such an immense love that it got reciprocated the same way by the Lord. As the Lord says, "Howsoever men seek Me, so do I respond to them."

Vrinda had once cursed Lord Vishnu when the Supreme appeared in Human form and she could not recognize Him. She converted the Lord to stone and we worship that form of the Lord as Shaligram. Lord Krishna and Vrinda's marriage is celebrated every year in Hindu temples.

Khirachora Gopinath Temple: God Keeps the Offering Preserved for His Devotee

Lord stole sweet rice for His devotee Madhavendra Puri

Temple name changed to Khirachora Temple – located near Kolkata.

Madhavendra Puri on a pilgrimage stopped at this temple and saw khir (sweet rice) being offered to Lord Krishna and wished for a bowl of khir.

Considering this an offence in his mind, he moved out of the temple and lay down to sleep under a tree. As was the custom, the priest gave all bowls of khir back to the devotees who offered them and nothing was kept in the temple. At night, the temple was closed and everybody went to sleep.

At night, Lord Krishna appeared in the dream of the priest. The Lord told him that He had hidden one bowl of khir under His dress and it should be given to Madhavendra Puri.

The priest reopened the temple at midnight. He found the bowl of khir and went around looking for the devotee, calling his name aloud and found him sleeping under a tree outside the temple. This was the same bowl that the devotee had wished for and then thought it was an offence.

As the Lord stole khir for the devotee, the temple name changed to Khirachora Temple, i.e., the Temple of the Thief of Khir.

Pagla Baba Mandir in Vrindavan: Lord Krishna Appears in Court As a Witness

This is a very recent story about an old devotee of Lord Krishna who was also a very poor man. He took loan from a financer and with lot of difficulty, he repaid the loan. In the villages in India, many people are not well educated and do not know how to do the paperwork and rely on faith and truthfulness.

When old man was about to repay the last instalment, the financer took him to the local court and said that his money had not been returned. The judge heard the case and asked the old man if he had anyone who witnessed him returning the money to the financer.

Pagla Baba Mandir in Vrindavan: Lord Krishna Appears in Court As a Witness

Old man said Bihari ji (Krishna), i.e., God was his witness. The judge, thinking that there was some person by the name of Bihariji, asked summons to be sent to him. The old man gave address of Bihari ji (Lord Krishna) temple in Vrindavan. The summons were sent. The summons were duly received. On the day of the hearing, when Bihariji's name was called, He appeared as an old man and gave the complete details of the dates when the instalments were paid. When checked, all the entries were found accurate. To cheat the old man, the financer had changed the name of the person from whom he had received the amounts on those dates. The old man was relieved but the judge became very curious and called him as he wanted to know about the witness. How did the witness, who was also an old man, remember everything so accurately? The judge thought the old man was joking when he said that he did not even recognize the person who had come as a witness. The judge asked the Police to investigate the matter. They reported that the summons were sent to the Lord Krishna temple in Vrindavan. The judge immediately left for the temple. In temple, the priest said that they did receive the summons. They regularly receive letters from devotees addressed to God and they keep them in front of Lord Krishna's idol. They did not know about any old man who may have gone from the temple to the court. When the judge checked, he found that the summons were still there in front of Lord Krishna's statue, unopened. The judge realized that the person who appeared in front of him in the court was Lord Krishna. He resigned his position and was spotted in Vrindavan singing ecstatically devotional songs of Lord Krishna. He is called Pagla Baba meaning a Saint who had gone insane due to his love for Lord Krishna. A huge temple was built by Pagla Baba due to his extreme devotion and love for Lord Krishna. Pagla Baba left his body in December 2021 at the age of 55.

Sakshi Gopal Mandir: God Travelled with His Devotee

This is a beautiful story where Lord Krishna appeared in a temple and then followed his devotee over a long distance to be a witness. The Lord travelled all the way from Vrindavan and this temple is in Jagannath Puri in Orissa.

The story goes like this:

There was a village in which there was a rich Brahmin family. An orphan boy, Mahindra, lived near their house. Mahindra grew up with the daughter of the rich Brahmin, Vasanti. They liked each other and wanted to get married. But the father wanted his daughter to marry a rich widower.

Mahindra left for Gopal ji Temple and started living there.

A few days later, Raghav, Vasanti's father, and some villagers went on a pilgrimage. Raghav fell ill on the way. Sukhvir, the man Raghav had proposed marrying his daughter to, abandoned him. Mahindra came to know about Raghav's illness. He brought him to the Gopal ji Temple and nursed him. Pleased by the service and care, Raghav promised the marriage of his daughter to Mahindra.

Later, when Raghav went back to his village, he changed his mind. Mahindra went to the village court on Vasanti's advice to seek justice. The court asked Mahindra if there was any witness to the promise made by Raghav.

Mahindra remembered there was an idol of Lord Krishna in the room Raghav had lived when he was sick. So he went back to the temple and asked God's idol to be the witness. The Lord appeared before him and agreed. The Lord asked Mahindra to start for the village and He would follow. But the Lord told him he should never look back. The journey was long, so Mahindra asked Him how he would know that the Lord is following him. The Lord said that Mahindra could listen to the sound of His anklets.

They travelled for few days. At one point when they crossed a river, sand got into the anklets and Mahindra did not hear their sound. So Mahindra got worried and looked back. The Lord was standing right behind him. The Lord smiled and then got firmly rooted there on the ground. The news spread about this event quickly. Everyone who heard about it came over. Soon a temple was made at the spot. Mahindra and Vasanti got married. Mahindra became the first priest and caretaker of the temple.

In the Bhagavad-Gita, the Lord says: I am the Witness sitting inside you as your Soul. He fulfils His promises to the devotees.

Nidhi Van (Vrindavan): Radha–Krishna Come Every Night, Even Today

Even today, it is believed that Lord Radha and Krishna appear every day in Nidhi van. There is a temple of Lord Krishna here. It is said that Lord Krishna used to dance here with His devotees. A number of devotees came on earth with the Lord. This place now has number of trees surrounding the temple. Lord Krishna and Radha come when it is dark. It is believed that the whole place gets illuminated when they arrive. All the trees become alive and take the form of Lord Krishna's devotees and the Lord dances with them through the night.

Nidhi Van (Vrindavan): Radha–Krishna Come Every Night, Even Today

Every day, the preparations are made in this temple for the Lord's appearance at night along with Radharani and other devotees. Food is prepared and kept; beds are decorated for the Lord to take rest; water is kept; shoes are kept and even datun to clean the teeth is kept. After evening, no one is allowed to stay near that place. In the past anyone who tried to stay became indisposed and was unable to reveal anything about what happened in the night. The houses facing that area close their windows and draw the curtains in the evening.

Once all preparations are complete, the temple is locked. One after the other, there are five doors that are locked. Then everyone leaves that place. There are many monkeys, birds and even dogs and other animals that roam around the temple and the small forest surrounding it during the day, but they all somehow have the intelligence that as the evening draws closer, they should all leave the place.

In the morning, when the temple is opened after opening the five locks one after the other, everything is used – food has been eaten, water has been drunk, datun has been used, shoes have been used, all the ornaments for Lord Radha (Lord Krishna's consort) have been used and bed has also been used.

Everything that is left over is distributed to devotees in the morning as prasad. This happens every day and has been happening for more than 5,000 years.

CHAPTER 10
Failure of Aspirant Yogi Is Success

Failure of Aspirant Yogi Is Success

- Lord Krishna's devotee never falls, never perishes.

- None who strives for self-redemption ever meets with evil destiny.

- The journey of the next birth starts from where the journey ended in the last birth.

- The supreme Human birth is birth in the family of Enlightened Yogis – most rare birth.

- Next to this rare birth is the birth in the family of rich and pious parents.

Failure of Aspirant Yogi Is Success

There is no fall for him either here or hereafter. For, O My beloved, none who strives for self-redemption (i.e., God-realization) ever meets with evil destiny – Lord Krishna – BG 6.40.

Destiny of Imperfect Yogi with Desires

First Heavenly Planets

then Birth in Rich and Pious Families

Such a person who has strayed from Yoga, obtains the higher worlds, (Heaven etc.) to which men of meritorious deeds alone are entitled, and having resided there for innumerable years, takes birth of pious and prosperous parents – Lord Krishna – BG 6.41.

Who takes birth in a rich family, though under the sway of his senses, feels drawn towards God by force of the habit acquired in his previous birth; nay, even the seeker of Yoga (in the form of even-mindedness) transcends the fruit of actions performed with some interested motive as laid down in the Vedas – Lord Krishna – BG 6.44.

Destiny of Imperfect Yogi with Dispassion

Birth in Enlightened Families – Rare Birth

(Defeats Journey to Heaven)

If he is possessed of dispassion, then not attaining to those regions (Heaven) he is born in the family of enlightened Yogis but such a birth in this world is very difficult to obtain – Lord Krishna – BG 6.42.

He automatically regains in that birth the latencies of even-mindedness of his previous birth; and through that he strives harder than ever for perfection in the form of God-Realization – Lord Krishna – BG 6.43.

Failure of Aspirant Yogi Is Success

- *The Yogi, however, who diligently takes up the practice, attains perfection in this very life with the help of latencies of many births, and being thoroughly purged of sin, forthwith reaches the Supreme state – Lord Krishna – BG 6.45.*
- *The Yogi is superior to ascetics; he is regarded superior even to those versed in sacred lore. The Yogi is also superior to those who perform action with some interested motive – Lord Krishna – BG 6.46.*

In the battlefield, Arjuna asks Lord Krishna – What happens to the Aspirant Yogi who follows your teachings but still could not perfect it in this birth because the mind is very powerful and very difficult to control. Is he not lost like a torn cloud who neither enjoyed the material pleasures nor could make it to God's Abode. Is he lost in the process?

Lord Krishna tells Arjuna that no one who strives for self-redemption (God realization) ever meets with evil destiny. He gets a very promising next birth (more promising environment) as a Human and he continues his spiritual journey from where he left in his last birth.

Lord Krishna says that there are two types of Aspirant Yogis who could not make to God's Abode and explains what happens to them.

The first type of Aspirant Yogi had some desires that he could not control. He is sent to Heaven to fulfil his desires because Heaven is place to fulfil the un-fulfilled desires. After residing there for some years, he takes birth with pious and prosperous parents. Notice the words of "pious and prosperous". So he has the environment that is promising and conducive to his onward spiritual journey. Parents are prosperous so he is not short of anything that is needed on earth. The Lord further says that the person imbibes knowledge and continues the onward journey with greater thrust. He is obviously a changed person now because he has already fulfilled his desires and is now free from them

Failure of Aspirant Yogi Is Success

The second type of Aspirant Yogi is the one who had no desires. So he is not sent to Heaven as Heaven is meaningless for him. He is immediately reborn in the family of enlightened Yogis. But Lord Krishna says that such a birth is very rare. The person has the most suitable environment and blessings to continue the journey. Remember, we mentioned that there are 400,000 types of Human births.

The Lord further states that since you know all these spiritual secrets now, why do you waste your life and time? You should aim to reach God's Abode within this birth because if you strive hard, all your past good Karmas from latencies of your past births will get amplified and come to your support to remove all your obstacles so you can make it within this birth itself.

- ❖ ***The Yogi, however, who diligently takes up the practice, attains perfection in this very life with the help of latencies of many births, and being thoroughly purged of sin, forthwith reaches the supreme state – Lord Krishna – BG 6.45.***

Sita Ram

CHAPTER 11

Manifest God and Un-manifest God

Manifest God, Un-manifest God and Spiritual Potency of the Lord

- Jnana (knowledge of the Absolute or Nirguna Brahma).
- Vijnana (knowledge of Sakara Brahma or manifest Divinity).
- Manifest God is incarnations that happen from time to time on the Planet Earth when God or His some spiritual form, is face-to-face with us.
- Un-manifest form is present around us all the time – Guiding, Listening, Recording and our Karmas will become latencies of past Karmas.
- Spiritual potency of the Lord runs these universes Above Time and Below Time.

Manifest Supreme, Un-manifest Supreme and Spiritual Potency of the Supreme

Manifest form of Supreme

Un-Manifest Form of Supreme That Nourishes All the Universes
Truth – Consciousness - Bliss

Spiritual Potency of Supreme

This knowledge (of both the Nirguna and Saguna aspects of Divinity) is a sovereign science, a sovereign secret, supremely holy, most excellent, directly enjoyable, attended with virtue, very easy to practise and imperishable – Lord Krishna – BG 9.2.

Manifest God

- Lord Krishna appeared on earth 5,200 years ago. He is the complete incarnation of the Supreme Personality of Godhead or He is God on earth.
- God manifests from time to time on Planet Earth. But His un-manifest form is all around us all the time with a thousand ears, a thousand eyes and face on every side.

Lord Radha–Krishna: God Manifests from Time to Time

यदा यदा हि धर्मस्य ग्लानिर्भवति भारत | अभ्युत्थानमधर्मस्य तदात्मानं सृजाम्यहम् ||
परित्राणाय साधूनां विनाशाय च दुष्कृताम् | धर्मसंस्थापनार्थाय सम्भवामि युगे युगे ||

- ❖ *Whenever there is a decline in righteousness and an increase in unrighteousness, O Arjuna, at that time I manifest myself on earth – Lord Krishna – BG 4.7.*

- ❖ *To protect the righteous, to annihilate the wicked, and to re-establish the principles of dharma I appear on this earth, age after age – Lord Krishna – BG 4.8.*

- ❖ *Hardly one among thousands of men strives to realize Me; of those striving Yogis, again, some rare one devoting himself exclusively to Me, knows Me in reality – Lord Krishna – BG 7.3.*

- ❖ *I am the supreme goal, sustainer, lord, witness, abode, refuge, well-wisher seeking no return, origin and end, resting-place, store-house to which all beings return at the time of universal destruction, and the imperishable seed – Lord Krishna – BG 9.18.*

Lord Krishna

Like clusters of yarn-beads formed by knots on a thread, all this is threaded on Me – Lord Krishna – BG 7.7.

I am life in all beings – Lord Krishna – BG 7.9.

I am the eternal seed of all beings. I am the intelligence of the intelligent – Lord Krishna – BG 7.10.

I am the radiance in the Moon and the Sun. I am the sacred syllable OM – Lord Krishna – BG 7.8.

I am the sound in ether – Lord Krishna – BG 7.8.

Adhiyajna, the Un-manifest Divinity dwelling in the heart of all beings as their Witness – Lord Krishna – BG 7.30.

Lord Krishna

The Supreme Spirit beyond the reach of mind and senses and embodiment of Truth, Consciousness and Bliss – Lord Krishna – BG 7.24.

The Supreme Spirit beyond the reach of mind and senses and Embodiment of Truth, Consciousness and Bliss – Lord Krishna – BG 7.24.

It is I who remain seated in the heart of all creatures as the inner controller of all – Lord Krishna – BG 15.15.

The radiance in the Sun that illumines the entire world, and that which shines in the Moon and that which shines in the fire too, know that radiance to be Mine – Lord Krishna – BG 15.12.

The Whole of this universe is permeated by Me as Un-manifest Divinity, like ice by water and all beings dwell on the idea within Me – Lord Krishna – BG 9.4.

Becoming the sapful Moon, I nourish all plants – Lord Krishna – BG 15.13.

Among calculators, I am Time – Lord Krishna – BG 10.30.

Lord Krishna

I am immortality as well as death; even so, I am being and also non-being – Lord Krishna – BG 9.19.

I am the supreme goal, lord, witness, abode, refuge, well-wisher seeking no return, origin and end, resting-place, store-house to which all beings return at the time of universal destruction, and the imperishable seed – Lord Krishna – BG 9.18.

I am the wisdom of the wise. I am goodness of the good – Lord Krishna – BG 10.36–10.38.

Of all knowledge, I am knowledge of the Soul (metaphysics) – Lord Krishna – BG 10.32.

I am the sustainer and ruler of this universe, its father, mother and grandfather, the one worth knowing, the purifier, the sacred syllable OM, and the three Vedas – Rig, Yajus and Sama – Lord Krishna – BG 9.17.

I am the Vedic ritual, I am the sacrifice, I am the offering to the departed; I am the herbage and food grains; I am the sacred mantra, I am the clarified butter, I am the sacred fire, and I am verily the act of offering oblation into the fire – Lord Krishna – BG 9.16.

Lord Krishna

Adhiyajna, Un-manifest Divinity seated in heart of all beings as the inner witness – Lord Krishna – BG 8.4.

I am the universal Self seated in the hearts of all beings – Lord Krishna – BG 10.20.

I am the consciousness (life-energy) in all beings – Lord Krishna – BG 10.22.

I am Vishnu among the twelve sons of Aditi, and the radiant Sun among the luminaries – Lord Krishna – BG 10.21.

I am Ksetrajna (individual Soul) in all the ksetras (fields) – Lord Krishna – BG 13.2.

I am Sri Rama – Lord Krishna – BG 10.31.

I am Shiva – Lord Krishna – BG 10.23.

I am Skanda – Lord Krishna – BG 10.24.

I am the prime cause in all respects of gods as well as of great seers – Lord Krishna – BG 10.2.

Lord Krishna

Supreme Has His Face on All Sides, Ears and Eyes All Around

Among sacrifices, I am the sacrifice of Japa (chanting) – Lord Krishna – BG 10.25.

I am Ganges – Lord Krishna – BG 10.23.

Of feminities, I am Kirti, Sri, Vak, Smrti, Medha, Dhrti and Ksama (the goddesses presiding over glory, prosperity, speech, memory, intelligence, fortitude and forbearance) – Lord Krishna – BG 10.34.

I am the sustainer of all having my face on all sides – Lord Krishna – BG 10.33.

I am the hymn known as Gayatri – Lord Krishna – BG 10.35.

Lord Krishna

Virat Darshan: All Gods and Existences in Lord Krishna – Seen by Arjuna

Arjuna saw the Supreme Deity possessing many mouths and eyes, presenting a wondrous sight, decked with many ornaments, wielding several uplifted divine weapons, wearing divine garlands and vestments, anointed all over with divine fragrances, full of wonders, infinite and having a face on all sides – BG 11.10–11.11.

You are the Supreme, Indestructible, Worthy of being known; You are the ultimate refuge of this universe. You are, again, the protector of the ageless Dharma; I consider You to be the eternal imperishable Being – Arjuna to Lord Krishna – BG 11.18.

Lord Krishna Is Sat, Asat and Beyond: Indestructible Brahma

- *O Infinite, O Lord of Celestials, O Abode of the universe, You are that which is existent (Sat), that which is non-existent (Asat) and also that which is beyond both, viz., the Indestructible Brahma – Arjuna to Lord Krishna – BG 11.37.*

- *You are the Father of this moving and unmoving creation, nay, the greatest teacher worthy of adoration. O Lord of incomparable might, in all the three worlds there is none else even equal to You; how can anyone be greater than You? – Arjuna to Lord Krishna – BG 11.43.*

Lord Krishna

Krishna Brings Full Security to His Devotees

अनन्याश्चिन्तयन्तो मां ये जनाः पर्युपासते | तेषां नित्याभियुक्तानां योगक्षेमं वहाम्यहम् ||

- ❖ *Those who worship Me in a disinterested spirit, to those ever united in thought with Me, I bring full security and personally attend to their needs – Lord Krishna – BG 9.22.*

- ❖ *Whosoever offers Me with love a leaf, a flower, a fruit or water, I appear in person before that selfless devotee of selfless mind, and delightfully partake of that article offered by him with love – Lord Krishna – BG 9.26.*

Ego Is More Powerful than Intelligence

- Mind is 10 times more powerful than gross body elements.

- Intelligence is 10 times more powerful than mind (mind can be controlled by intelligence).

- Ego is 10 times more powerful than Intelligence (only surrender to the Lord can control the ego).

- ❖ **Earth, water, fire, air, ether, mind, reason and also ego – these constitute My Nature divided into eight parts. This indeed is My lower (material) Nature; other than this, by which the whole universe is sustained, know it to be My higher (or spiritual) Nature in the form of Jiva (the life-principle) – Lord Krishna – BG 7.4–7.5.**

Lord's Lower Nature and Higher Nature

Lower Nature of Lord

➢ Earth, Water, Fire, Air, Ether – Gross Body – only for this birth.

➢ Mind, Intelligence, Ego – Subtle Body – travels from one body to the next and decides the future birth with Karmas.

Higher Nature of Lord

➢ Soul – Higher Nature – complete God's presence in us – Guide, Nourisher, Witness.

Faith Decides the Destination

My Devotee never perishes – Lord Krishna – BG 9.31.

- ❖ *Those who are votaries of gods, go to gods; those who are votaries of manes, reach the manes; those who adore the spirits, reach the spirits and those who worship Me, come to Me alone – Lord Krishna – BG 9.25.*

- ➢ Our faith plays a very important role in our Human lives and decides our next destination. Whatever is the Nature of our faith, our Karmas happen accordingly and firm up our destination.

- ❖ *Thinking of whatever entity one leaves the body at the time of death, that and that alone one attains, being ever absorbed in its thought – Lord Krishna – BG 8.6.*

Manifest and Un-Manifest Divinity

Above Time

Below Time: Three Gunas – Satvik, Rajasik, Tamasic　　

- ❖ *The whole of this universe is permeated by Me as Un-manifest Divinity, like ice by water and all beings dwell in the idea within Me – Lord Krishna – BG 9.4.*

- ❖ *During the Final Dissolution all beings enter My Prakriti (the Prime Cause), and at the beginning of creation, I send them forth again according to their respective Karmas and subject to the sway of their Nature – Lord Krishna – BG 9.7–9.8.*

- ➢ Our Nature and Karmas stay with us even when all the universes are destroyed. They ride on our personal identity (Soul) which is fragment of the Lord. Even after the Final Dissolution, our next birth is decided by our Karmas and Nature. Soul is important in our life-to-life journey. All this knowledge would not have come to us if the Lord had not revealed the Bhagavad-Gita. That is why Lord Krishna said in chapter 4 that He revealed this supreme secret to the Sun-god and for a long time, this secret had gone missing from this earth and same had been revealed again to Arjuna and to all of us.

All souls draw life energy from God – There is no one in-between you and God. God is the only one who can give shelter and liberation. Guru can guide you to God's path but your own karmas will decide your destination.

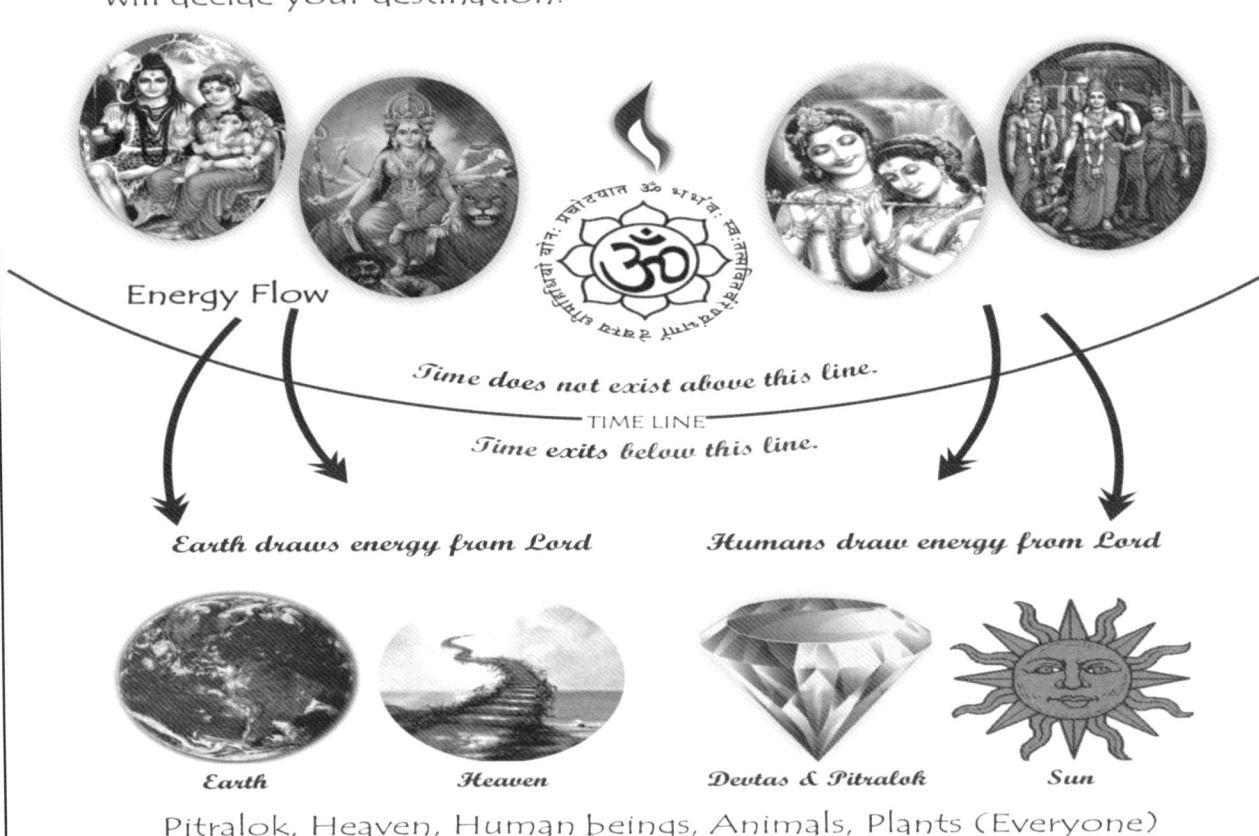

Pitralok, Heaven, Human beings, Animals, Plants (Everyone) draws energy directly from Lord. Imagine the one who moves earth around sun at a speed more than 100,000 km. per hour.

CHAPTER 12

Yogamaya: The Spiritual Potency of the Supreme

Yogamaya: The Spiritual Potency of the Supreme

- Yogamaya appeared along with Lord Krishna on same day in the home of Nand and Yashoda
- Yogamaya is the Spiritual Potency and sister of Lord Krishna.
- Yogamaya resides on Vindhayachal and is also known as Vindhyavasini.
- Yogamaya is always with Lord Krishna and protects Lord Krishna from the three Gunas.

Yogamaya: The Spiritual Potency of the Supreme

- ❖ ***Veiled by My Yogamaya, My divine potency, I am not manifest to all – Lord Krishna – BG 7.25.***
- ➢ Yogamaya is Krishna's Spiritual Potency. She is Above Time but appears with Lord Krishna when the Lord comes on earth. When the Lord was born, she also appeared as the daughter of Nand and Yashoda.
- ➢ Yogamaya is Mahamaya below Time. She is also called Maya and governs the complete universe. The Planetary System is just one part of her universe. Lord Krishna also mentions that His Maya is very strong and is too difficult to break through. The only way to get out of this is worship of Lord Krishna.
- ➢ Maya keeps us engaged and lost throughout life. That is why the Lord mentions that He is not manifest to all. This means the devotees who love and worship Krishna can know His manifestation as Yogamaya will allow them to know Lord Krishna.
- ❖ ***I appear in Human form through My Yogamaya for deliverance of the world – Lord Krishna – BG 9.11.***
- ❖ ***Though birthless and immortal and the Lord of all beings, I manifest Myself through My own Yogamaya (Divine Potency), keeping my Nature under control – Lord Krishna – BG 4.6.***
- ➢ The same Goddess as Yogamaya runs the universes Above Time and as Mahamaya runs the universes Below Time.

Yogamaya: The Spiritual Potency of the Supreme – Daughter of Nand and Yashoda

When God appears on this earth taking a form that is visible to Humans, He has manifested. However God is present all around us all the time with a thousand eyes, a thousand hands and ears as per Bhagavad-Gita, which is the way to explain that God is the True Guide as well as witness to everything that is happening.

God is present in everyone in their heart. Learned and enlightened Yogis see Lord in everyone – Humans, Animals and others.

Though birthless and immortal and the Lord of all beings, I manifest Myself through My own Yogamaya (Divine Potency), keeping My Nature (Prakriti) under control – Lord Krishna – BG 4.6.

Here the reference is to Yogamaya, the Spiritual Potency of the Lord. Yogamaya is the divine potency that has form of goddess Durga. The same goddess governs the spiritual worlds Above Time as Yogamaya and worlds Below Time as Mahamaya.

Even when the Lord manifests, everyone does not know Him. It is only a few worthy, pious devotees that realize Him. The rest consider Him as an ordinary Human Being.

Yogamaya is the curtain that does not let everyone realize the presence of God. Mother Durga was worshipped by gopis in the form of Yogamaya as they had no material desires and just wanted to be with Lord Krishna all the time. Yogamaya takes the true, desireless and pious devotees to Lord Krishna.

Yogamaya: The Spiritual Potency of the Supreme – Daughter of Nand and Yashoda

The Mahamaya form runs the universes Below Time and bewilders the people and keeps them engaged in mundane activities. Ones who are pure and desireless are guided by Mahamaya to the spiritual path to Yogamaya and to Lord Krishna.

Both Yogamaya and Mahamaya are the same – it is just that one is the Spiritual Potency and the other is the Material Potency of Lord Krishna. The same Shakti goddess plays both the roles. She raises the devotees, uplifts them to God in one form and in the other form keeps the impure and non-devotees away from Him. She keeps the impure and non-devotees occupied in their ego and makes them go through repeated cycles of births and rebirths.

Mother Yogamaya as visualized by enlightened Yogi, Yogananda ji is shown in the picture here. When Lord Krishna took birth as the son of Vasudeva and mother Devaki, the Lord advised mother Yogamaya to appear on earth also, as the daughter of Nand and Yashoda. Both the children appeared on the same day and the children were exchanged.

Mother Yogamaya flew to the sky and appeared in her eight-armed form. Mother Yogamaya did not continue her childhood along with Lord Krishna. Lord Krishna and mother Yogamaya are brother and sister when they appear on earth.

Krishna Radha

CHAPTER 13

Un-manifest God: Brahma – Infinite Consciousness

Un-manifest God: Brahma – Infinite Consciousness

सर्वत: पाणिपादं तत्सर्वतोऽक्षिशिरोमुखम् | सर्वत: श्रुतिमल्लोके सर्वमावृत्य तिष्ठति ||

He has hands and feet on all sides, eyes, head and mouth in all directions, and ears all around, for he stands pervading all in the universe – Lord Krishna explains about Brahma – BG 13.14.

- Un-manifest God – Infinite Consciousness
- Truth – Consciousness – Bliss
- Always blessing
- Same to all

Brahma or Indestructible:
Un-manifest Supreme Is Present Everywhere

Truth, Consciousness and Bliss – Bhagavad-Gita

Nature of Brahma is very well explained here:

Truth – It is "Truth". It is the real truth. It has always been the real truth and it will always be the real truth. Even when all the worlds will be destroyed, Brahma will still exist. There is no place without Brahma.

Consciousness – It is best explained by saying that it has thousand eyes, thousand ears and face on all sides. We can not see but Brahma is seeing us all the time, guiding us, coaching us but is also witness to whatever we do.

Bliss – Nature is that it is always blessing. We do good Karmas or bad Karmas, it is always blessing us because that is the Nature of Brahma.

Triple Appellation of Brahma: OM, TAT and SAT

Truth, Consciousness and Bliss – Bhagavad-Gita

- *OM–TAT–SAT has been declared as triple appellation of Brahma, who is Truth, Consciousness and Bliss. By that were the Brahmanas and the Vedas as well as sacrifices created at the Cosmic Dawn – Lord Krishna – BG 17.23.*

- *Acts of sacrifice, charity and austerity, as enjoined by sacred precepts, are always commenced by noble persons, used to recitation of Vedic chants, with the invocation of the divine name OM – Lord Krishna – BG 17.24.*

- *With the idea that all this belongs to God, who is denoted by the appellation TAT, acts of sacrifice and austerity as well as acts of charity of various kinds, are performed by the seekers of liberation, expecting no return for them – Lord Krishna – BG 17.25.*

- *The name of God SAT is also used in the sense of reality and goodness. And the word SAT is also used in the sense of praiseworthy, auspicious action. And steadfastness in sacrifice, austerity and charity is likewise spoken of as SAT and action for the sake of God is verily termed as SAT – Lord Krishna – BG 17.26.*

Brahma or Indestructible: Un-manifest – Nature of Brahma Is Undefinable

Sat – Chit – Anand
Truth – Consiousness – Bliss

Truth, Consciousness and Bliss – Bhagavad-Gita

- **Unthinkable**
- **Omnipresent**
- **Indestructible**
- **Indefinable**
- **Eternal**
- **Immovable**
- **Un-manifest**
- **Changeless**

– Lord Krishna – BG 12.3–12.4.

Supreme Brahma is the Lord of the two beginningless entities – Prakriti and Jiva (individual Soul) – is said to be neither Sat (being) nor Asat (non-being) – Lord Krishna – BG 13.12.

It has hands and feet on all sides; eyes, head and mouth in all directions; and ears all-round; for it stands pervading all in the universe – Lord Krishna – BG 13.13.

Though perceiving all sense-objects it is, really speaking, devoid of all senses. Nay, though unattached, it is the sustainer of all nonetheless; and though attribute-less, it is the enjoyer of Gunas, the three modes of Prakriti – Lord Krishna – BG 13.14.

- Lord Krishna has explained about the Un-manifest in a number of ways. The Lord says it is "indefinable" so all our efforts will not succeed in defining the real Brahma. It is basically the presence of the Lord all around us, inside us, Below Time and Above Time in a form that we cannot see. Even the minutest of our Karmas get watched and recorded.

Absolute Is Untouched by Evil and Is the Same to All

- *The omnipresent God does not partake the virtue or sin of anyone. Knowledge is enveloped by ignorance; hence beings are constantly falling a prey to delusion – Lord Krishna – BG – 5.15.*

- *Absolute is untouched by evil and is the same to all – Lord Krishna – BG 5.19.*

- *Those wise men who are free from lust and anger, who have subdued their mind and have realized God, Brahma, the abode of eternal peace, is present all-round – Lord Krishna – BG 5.26.*

- *My primordial Nature, known as the great Brahma, is the womb of all creatures. In that womb I place the seed of all life. The creation of all beings follows from that union of Matter and Spirit – Lord Krishna – BG 14.3.*

- *Of all embodied beings that appear in all the species of various kinds, Arjuna, Prakriti or Nature is the conceiving Mother, while I am the seed-giving Father – Lord Krishna – BG 14.4.*

Absolute is the same to All. Absolute does not differentiate. Absolute is always blessing. Guru Nanak ji also worshipped on the Absolute form. Absolute is same to all and our individual Soul survives and lives in this world with a personal identity – a fragment of Lord Krishna.

Brahma or Indestructible: Un-manifest Is Supreme

❖ *He exists without and within all beings and constitutes the moving and the unmoving creation as well. And by reason of its subtlety, it is incomprehensible; it is close at hand yet stands afar too – Lord Krishna – BG 13.15.*

❖ *Though integral like space in its undivided aspect, it appears divided as it were, in all animate and inanimate beings. And that Godhead, which is the only one worth knowing, is the sustainer of beings (as Vishnu), the destroyer (as Rudra) and the creator of all (as Brahma) – Lord Krishna – BG 13.16.*

In the Bhagavad-Gita, Lord Krishna says that same un-manifest God is the only one worth knowing. The Lord says that same Godhead is Brahma, the creator of the universe; Vishnu, the sustainer of the universe; and Shiva, the destroyer of the universe. The same Lord takes these forms and performs the actions.

Brahma or Indestructible: Un-manifest – Nature of Brahma

- ❖ *That supreme Brahma is said to be the light of all lights and entirely beyond Maya. That Godhead is knowledge itself, worth knowing, and worth attaining through real wisdom, and is particularly abiding in the hearts of all – Lord Krishna – BG 13.17.*

- ➢ The same Lord is present in our heart also; it is the fragment of same Lord. The same Lord is present in a visible form in Brahma (Creator of the universe), Vishnu and Shiva and the same Lord is also present in us. We can rise to Lord's Abode by purifying ourselves – our Mind, our Nature and our Karmas.

- ❖ *The moment man perceives the diversified existence of beings as rooted in the one supreme Spirit, and the spreading forth of all beings from the same, that very moment he attains Brahma (who is Truth, Consciousness and Bliss personified) – Lord Krishna – BG 13.30.*

- ➢ The Lord says that when this realization takes place that everything is rooted in the same Lord, with that level of purity, one is able to identify oneself with Brahma or OM.
  Brahma (OM) is different from Brahman (Creator of the universe)

Brahma Possesses a Form beyond Human Conception

- *In this body, I am myself dwelling as the inner witness, am Adhiyajna – Lord Krishna – BG 8.4.*
- *Supreme Indestructible is Brahman. One's own Self (the Individual Soul) is called Adhyatama – Lord Krishna – BG 8.3.*
- *Brahman – all knowing, ageless being, the ruler of all, subtler than the subtle, the universal sustainer, ==possessing a form beyond Human conception,== effulgent like the Sun and far beyond the darkness of ignorance – Lord Krishna – BG 8.9.*
- *Supreme Goal – God who is an embodiment of Truth, Consciousness and Bliss, termed as Indestructible – Lord Krishna – BG 8.11.*
- *One Indestructible is OM – Lord Krishna – BG 8.12.*

> Our own Self, our personal identity in the Soul as fragment of Lord Krishna is termed as Adhyatama.

> Lord Krishnas personal presence in our body is termed as Adhiyajna. That is where the devotees realize His presence in their hearts.

> The Lord says that the form of Brahma is beyond Human conception. Earlier also Lord said that Brahma is indefinable.

Brahman according to Advaita and Dvaita schools of thought:

In Advaita Vedanta, Brahman is without attributes and strictly impersonal. It can be best described as Infinite Being, Infinite Consciousness and Infinite Bliss. It is the pure knowledge itself, similar to a source of Infinite Radiance.

OM and Indestructible Brahma

OM, all pervading light that emerges in Golok and spreads down to all the existences Above Time and then crosses the Viraja River that demarcates the existences Above Time and Below Time and comes down to the universes and mundane worlds. This light is mentioned by Lord Krishna as "Truth, Consciousness and Bliss Solidified" in the Bhagavad-Gita.

a) This light is "Truth" as it emerged from Lord Krishna. In Bhagavad-Gita, **Lord Krishna stated in verse 14.29 that "I am Substratum of Indestructible Brahma and immutable Bliss."**

b) This light has Consciousness. **It is mentioned in the Bhagavad-Gita that the All-Pervading Brahma has thousands of Eyes, Ears, Hands and Mouths and is spread in all the worlds Above and Below Time and is nourishing all.**

c) This light is "Bliss Solidified". This light is always blessing, more so to those engaged in pious activities and more so to the devotees and worshippers.

This Brahma is different from the Brahma who is the Creator of the universes. This Brahma that is addressed the same way is the light of OM and Paramatma.

Krishna: Substratum of Imperishable Unmanifest Brahma

ब्रह्मणो हि प्रतिष्ठहममृतस्याव्ययस्य च ।शाश्वतस्य च धर्मस्य सुखस्यैकान्तिकस्य च ॥

- *I am the Substratum of the imperishable Brahma, of immortality, of the eternal Dharma and of unending immutable bliss – Lord Krishna – BG 14.27.*

Krishna, who is known as Govinda, is the Supreme Godhead. He has an eternal blissful body. He is the origin of all. He has no other origin and He is the prime cause of all causes. Lord Brahma reveals in the Brahma Samhita which is written by Lord Brahma (Creator of the universe) that Lord Krishna is Substratum and source of un-manifest God which is realized by pious devotees as OM. This also means that the source of Un-manifest is Krishna in the manifest form. This un-manifest then takes a number of forms as it passes through the universes. Here we can remember again the lines from Brahma Samhita written by Lord Brahma when he was given the vision by Mother Saraswati.

Krishna, who is also known as Govinda, is the Supreme Godhead. He has an eternal blissful body. He is the origin of all. He has no other origin and He is the prime cause of all causes.– **Lord Brahma (Creator of the universe) in Sri Brahma Samhita**

Worshippers of Brahman Also Reach Krishna

ये त्वक्षरमनिर्देश्यमव्यक्तं पर्युपासते । सर्वत्रगमचिन्त्यञ्च कूटस्थमचलन्ध्रुवम् ॥
सन्नियम्येन्द्रियग्रामं सर्वत्र समबुद्धयः । ते प्राप्नुवन्ति मामेव सर्वभूतहिते रताः ॥

Those who constantly adore the unthinkable, omnipresent, indestructible, indefinable, eternal, immovable, Un-manifest and changeless Brahma, they too come to Me – Lord Krishna – BG 12.3–12.4.

The Lord answers a question of Arjuna about the destination of the people who worship only the Un-manifest. The Lord clarifies that those who are attached to the Un-manifest also reach Krishna. Because Krishna is the source of Un-manifest, so those worshippers will also reach the source.

Strain Is Greater for Those Attached to the Unmanifest

क्लेशोऽधिकतरस्तेषामव्यक्तासक्तचेतसाम् | अव्यक्ता हि गतिर्दुःखं देहवद्भिरवाप्यते ||

The strain is greater for those who have their mind attached to the Un-manifest, as attachment with the Un-manifest is attained with difficulty by the body-conscious people – Lord Krishna – BG 12.5.

The Lord clarifies that strain is greater for those who are attached to the Un-manifest because we are in a body and can relate easily if the form and source is in the same form as we are. Also, Un-manifest is impersonal, as stated earlier, and same to all.

Quoting from a write-up – The jñānīs who worship God as nirguṇa, nirviśheṣh, and nirākār, have to rely entirely upon self-effort for progress. ==On the other hand, the personal form of God is an ocean of compassion and mercy.== Hence, devotees of the personal form receive the help of divine support in their sādhanā. On the basis of the protection that God bestows upon His devotees, Sri Krishna stated in verse 9.31: "O son of Kunti, declare it boldly that my devotee never perishes."

Uttering OM (Formless) and Dwelling on Krishna (in Form)

ओमित्येकाक्षरं ब्रह्म व्याहरन्मामनुस्मरन् । यः प्रयाति त्यजन्देहं स याति परमां गतिम् ॥

One who departs from the body while remembering Me, the Supreme Personality, and chanting the syllable OM, will attain the supreme goal – Lord Krishna – BG 8.13.

CHAPTER 14

Cosmic Day and Cosmic Night

Cosmic Day and Cosmic Night: Time Check

इदं ज्ञानमुपाश्रित्य मम साधर्म्यमागताः |
सर्गेऽपि नोपजायन्ते प्रलये न व्यथन्ति च ||

Those who take refuge in this wisdom will be united with Me. They will not be reborn at the time of creation nor destroyed at the time of dissolution – Lord Krishna – BG 14.2.

➢ Brahma's one day is equal to a thousand Mahayugas.
➢ Brahma's one night is equal to a thousand Mahayugas.
➢ This is the reality of Time.

Creation and Destruction of Universes: Cosmic Day and Cosmic Night

❖ ***Far beyond this Un-manifest, there is yet another Un-manifest Existence, that Supreme Divine Person, who does not perish even though all beings perish – Lord Krishna – BG 8.20.***

 Above Time: No rebirth – No impact of Time

 Below Time: Subject to birth and re-birth with Time

All embodied beings emanate from the Un-manifest (Brahma's subtly body) at the beginning of the cosmic day; at the cosmic nightfall, they merge into the same subtle body as Brahma, known as the un-manifest – Lord Krishna – BG 8.18.

Lord Brahma, the creator of the universes, is un-manifest but the Lord also has an age of 100 years. His one day is equal to millions of years on earth. When after 100 years, Lord Brahma (creator) also ceases to exist, Life Above Time and Lord Krishna as Manifest and un-manifest still exist. Because the creator Lord Brahma is Below Time, there has to be a day when everything Below Time has to cease, except our Souls that migrate at that time.

Final Dissolution: Everything Merges in Krishna; Karmas Still Hold On to the Soul

सहस्रयुगपर्यन्तमहर्यद्ब्रह्मणो विदुः । रात्रिं युगसहस्रान्तां तेऽहोरात्रविदो जनाः ॥

One day of Brahma (kalp) lasts a thousand cycles of the four ages (mahā yug) and His night also extends for the same span of time. The wise who know this understand the reality about day and night – Lord Krishna – BG 8.17.

During the Final Dissolution all beings enter My Prakriti (the prime cause), and at the beginning of creation, I send them forth again – Lord Krishna – BG 9.7.

Wielding My Nature I procreate again and again, according to their respective Karmas, all this multitude of beings subject to the sway of their own Nature – Lord Krishna – BG 9.8.

CHAPTER 15

Three Gunas:
Three Destinations

Three Gunas: Three Destinations

पुरुषः प्रकृतिस्थो हि भुङ्क्ते प्रकृतिजान्गुणान् | कारणं गुणसङ्गोऽस्य सदसद्योनिजन्मसु ||

It is the attachment with these Gunas that is responsible for the birth of this Soul in good and evil wombs – Lord Krishna – BG 13.21.

- Life after Life: Heavenly Abodes, Human Birth or Hellish Planets
- Fourth Destination: God's Abode – Above Time
- Above Time: No birth, No Death, No old age, No disease

- **When a man dies during the preponderance of Sattva, he obtains the stainless ethereal worlds (heaven etc.) attained by men of noble deeds – Lord Krishna – BG 14.14.**

- **Dying when Rajas predominates, he is born among those attached to action; even so, the man who has expired during the preponderance of Tamas is reborn in the species of the deluded creatures such as insects and beasts etc. – Lord Krishna – BG 14.15.**

Mother Sita: Humble Appearance on Earth as Consort of the Supreme Lord Rama

Three Gunas: Three Destinations – Heaven, Human Birth, Hellish Planets

Sattva, Rajas and Tamas: these three Gunas born of Nature tie down the imperishable Soul to the body – Lord Krishna – BG 14.5.

These three Gunas fight for their Supremacy – Lord Krishna – BG 14.10.

Gunas	Sattva (Quality of Goodness)	Rajas (Principle of Activity)	Tamas (Principle of Inertia)
Destination after Death	Stainless ethereal worlds, e.g., Heavenly Planets	Human Birth	Insects and beasts
Leads to	Wisdom	Wisdom	Obstinate error and Stupor
	illuminating and flawless: binds through attachment to happiness and knowledge – Lord Krishna – BG 14.6.	Nature of Passion: born of desire and attachment, binds the Soul through attachment to actions and their fruit – Lord Krishna –BG 14.7.	Deluder of all those who look upon the body as their own Self, as born of ignorance, binds the Soul through error, sloth and sleep –Lord Krishna – BG- 14.8.
Result	Draws one to Joy	Draws one to Action	Draws one to error
	Light and discernment dawn in the body, mind and senses when Sattva prevails.	Greed, activity, undertaking of action with interested motive; restlessness, thirst for enjoyment make their appearance.	Obtuseness of the mind and senses, disinclination to perform one's obligatory duties, frivolity and stupor prevail.
Guna Domination	Soul wends its way upwards	Stays in the middle	Sinks down

Untutored Faith: Sattvik, Rajasic and Tamasic

Faith of all men conforms to their mental disposition. Faith constitutes a man; whatever the Nature of his faith, verily he is that – Lord Krishna – BG 17.3.

Gunas	Sattva (Quality of Goodness)	Rajas (Principle of Activity)	Tamas (Principle of Inertia)
Faith	Worship Gods	Worship demigods	Worship spirits of dead and ghosts
Food likings	Foods which promote longevity, intelligence, vigour, health, happiness and cheerfulness – naturally agreeable	Bitter, sour, salty, over-hot, pungent, dry and burning, and which cause suffering, grief and sickness	Ill cooked, not fully ripe, insipid, putrid, stale and polluted and which is impure too
Spirit of sacrifice	Follow scriptures, expect no return and believe that the sacrifices must be performed	Sacrifice offered for the sake of mere show or even with an eye to its fruit	Not in conformity with scriptural injunctions, no food is offered, no sacrificial fee is paid, no sacred chant of hymns, devoid of faith
Penance of body	Worship of gods, elders, great souls, purity, straightforwardness, continence and non-violence	Austerity for selfish gains	Intent to harm others
Penance of speech	Words which cause no annoyance to others, truthful, agreeable, beneficial, study of scriptures, chanting of divine names	Speech which is not pleasant and driven to get the material objectives	Speech to harm others and not advocated by scriptures
Penance of mind	Cheerfulness of mind, placidity, contemplation on God, control of mind, perfect purity of inner feelings	Mind wanders around material objectives	Mind works to harm others and engage in sinful activities

Domination at the Time of Death Decides Future Destination

Acts of sacrifice, charity and penance are purifiers to the wise men – Lord Krishna – BG 18.5.

Gunas	Sattva (Quality of Goodness)	Rajas (Principle of Activity)	Tamas (Principle of Inertia)
Knowledge	Man perceives one imperishable divine existence as undivided and equally present in all individual beings – Lord Krishna – BG 18.20.	Man cognizes many existences of various kinds, as apart from one another, in all beings	Clings to one body as if it were the whole – which is irrational, has no real grasp of truth and is trivial
Action	Action which is ordained by the scriptures and is not accompanied by the sense of doership and has been done without attachment by one who seeks no return	Action which involves much strain and is performed by one who seeks enjoyments or by a man full of egotism	Action which is undertaken through sheer ignorance, without regard to consequences or loss to oneself, injury to others or one's own resourcefulness
Doer	Free from attachment, not egoistic, endowed with firmness and zeal and not swayed by success or failure	Free from attachment, not egoistic, endowed with firmness and zeal and not swayed by success or failure	Lacking piety and self-control, uncultured, arrogant, deceitful, inclined to rob others of their livelihood, slothful, despondent and procrastinating
Intellect	Correctly determines the paths of activity and renunciation, what should be done and what should not be done, what is fear and what is fearlessness, what is bondage and what is liberation	Does not truly perceive what is Dharma and what is Adharma, what ought to be done and what should not be done	Intellect wrapped in ignorance, which imagines even Adharma to be Dharma, and sees all other things upside-down

What It Tastes Is Not What It Results In
(Also, Even Gods Are Impacted)

There is no being on earth, or in the middle region or even among the gods or anywhere else, who is free from three Gunas, born of Prakriti – Lord Krishna – BG 18.40.

Gunas	Sattva (Quality of Goodness)	Rajas (Principle of Activity)	Tamas (Principle of Inertia)
Joy	The striver finds enjoyment through practise of adoration, meditation and service to God, whereby he reaches the end of sorrow – such a joy, though appearing as poison in the beginning, tastes like nectar in the end; hence that joy, born as it is of the placidity of mind brought about by meditation on God, has been declared as sattvik.	Delight, which ensues from the contact of the senses with their objects, is eventually poison-like, though appearing at first as nectar.	That which stupefies the Self during its enjoyment as well as in the end, derived from sleep, indolence and obstinate error, such delight has been called Tamasic.

It is the attachment with the three Gunas that is responsible for the birth of this Soul in good or evil wombs – Lord Krishna – BG 13.21.

दैवी ह्येषा गुणमयी मम माया दुरत्यया |
मामेव ये प्रपद्यन्ते मायामेतां तरन्ति ते ||

My divine energy Maya, consisting of the three modes of Nature, is very difficult to overcome. But those who surrender unto me cross over it easily – Lord Krishna – BG 7.14.

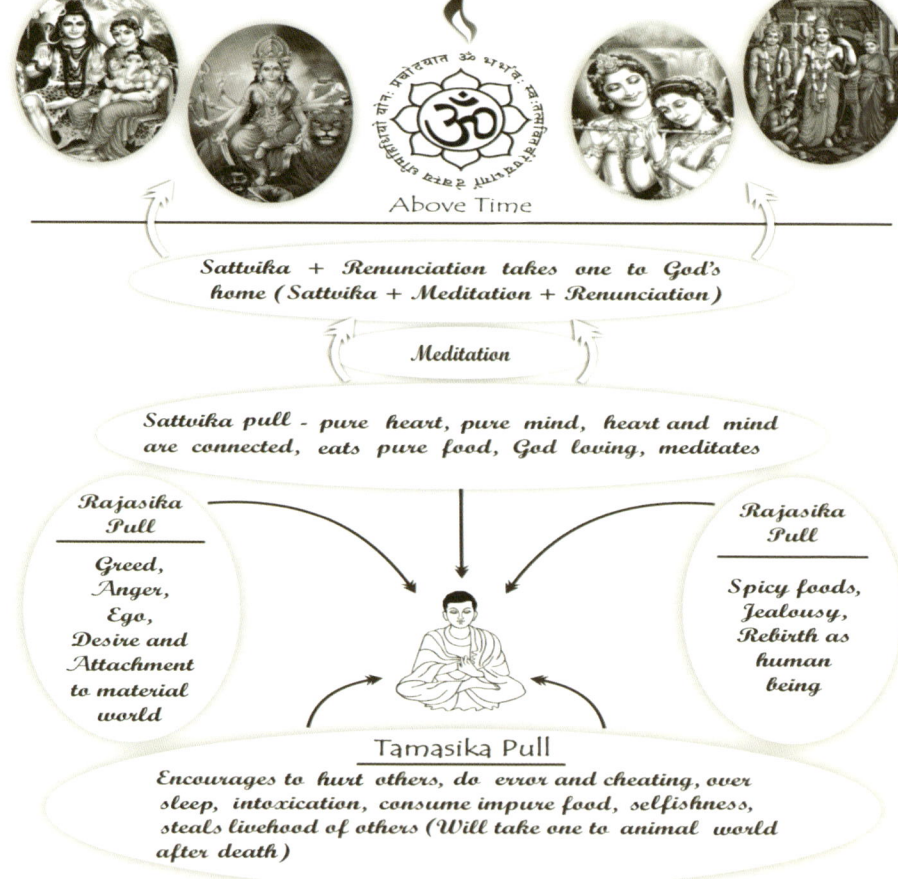

Human being is pulled by Sattvika, Rajasika and Tamasika all the time

CHAPTER 16

Lord Narayana: The Primeval Being

Lord Narayana: The Primeval Being

ततः पदं तत्परिमार्गितव्यं यस्मिन्गता न निवर्तन्ति भूयः । तमेव चाद्यं पुरुषं प्रपद्ये यतः प्रवृत्तिः प्रसृता पुराणी ॥

The Supreme Lord, from whom streamed forth the activity of the universe a long time ago, upon taking refuge in Him, one will not return to this world again – Lord Krishna – BG 15.4.

➢ Lord Krishna of Golok takes the form of Narayana in Hari Dham.
➢ All universes and incarnations progress from Lord Narayana.

Neither the Sun nor the Moon nor fire can illumine that supreme self-effulgent state, attaining which men do not return to this world; that is My supreme abode – Lord Krishna – BG 15.6.

God Talks to Arjuna towards the End of Bhagavad-Gita: Follow the Sequence

मच्चित्तः सर्वदुर्गाणि मत्प्रसादात्तरिष्यसि | अथ चेत्वमहङ्कारान्न श्रोष्यसि विनङ्क्ष्यसि ||

Lord Krishna says to Arjuna as the Lord concluded Bhagavad-Gita: With your mind devoted to Me, you shall, ==by My grace,== overcome all difficulties. But if from self-conceit you do not care to listen to Me, you will be lost – Lord Krishna – BG 18.58.

This sequence of conversations towards the end of Bhagavad-Gita is very revealing. Lord Krishna advises Arjuna to listen to the Lord. The Lord reveals that the only reason someone does not listen is due to ego. The Lord also reveals that with His grace, Arjuna can overcome all difficulties.

यदहङ्कारमाश्रित्य न योत्स्य इति मन्यसे | मिथ्यैष व्यवसायस्ते प्रकृतिस्त्वां नियोक्ष्यति ||

If, taking your stand based on egotism, you think, "I will not fight", vain is this resolve of yours; Nature will drive you to the act – Lord Krishna – BG 18.59.

The Lord tells Arjuna that If Arjuna decides not to fight, then this decision is coming out of his ego. His decision of not to fight will not work because Arjuna is a warrior by Nature. This is an unsolicited war, to bring righteousness on earth. This set of dialogues is very spiritual.

स्वभावजेन कौन्तेय निबद्धः स्वेन कर्मणा | कर्तुं नेच्छसि यन्मोहात्करिष्यस्यवशोऽपि तत् ||

That action, too, which you are not willing to undertake through ignorance you will ==perforce perform,== bound by your own duty, born of your Nature – Lord Krishna – BG 18.60.

The Lord says to Arjuna: If you are unwilling to perform this natural duty of yours (i.e., fighting this righteous war), it is your ignorance and not a wise decision. But the Lord further reveals that even if Arjuna was planning to take that decision (i.e., not to fight), his decision would not work as he would perforce perform the action bound by his own duty. Now what is that perforce? It will be clear in the next verse.

Karmas Revolve Us as If We Are Mounted on a Machine

ईश्वरः सर्वभूतानां हृद्देशेऽर्जुन तिष्ठति | भ्रामयन्सर्वभूतानि यन्त्रारूढानि मायया ||

God abides in the hearts of all creatures, causing them to revolve according to their Karma by His illusive power (Maya) as though mounted on a machine – Lord Krishna – BG 18.61.

We are all mounted on a machine. This machine runs as decided by the Lord and the Lord's system, and the Lord decides as per our own Karmas. So Karmas again come in the forefront here. Here Lord is revealing to Arjuna that He has chosen him for the task yet the Lord will actually perform the task. The Lord is seated in the hearts of all creatures.

तमेव शरणं गच्छ सर्वभावेन भारत | तत्प्रसादात्परां शान्तिं स्थानं प्राप्स्यसि शाश्वतम् ||

Take refuge in Him alone with all your being, Arjuna. By His mere grace you will attain supreme peace and the eternal abode – Lord Krishna – BG 18.62.

The Lord again advises Arjuna – which is the main message of Bhagavad-Gita – to surrender to the Lord and that surrender is the only way to get peace and eternal Abode which is the wish of every devotee. He should surrender and perform all his duties.

सर्वधर्मान्परित्यज्य मामेकं शरणं व्रज | अहं त्वां सर्वपापेभ्यो मोक्षयिष्यामि मा शुचः ||

Resigning all your duties to Me, the all-powerful and all supporting Lord, take refuge in Me alone: I shall absolve you of all sins, worry not – Lord Krishna – BG 18.66.

CHAPTER 17

Bhagavad-Gita:
An Astrological Aspect

Bhagavad-Gita: An Astrological Aspect

Astrology is the science which deals with the effects of planets of the solar system on all aspects in the life of an individual, as opposed to the science of Astronomy which merely deals with the physical properties of the planets.

- Vedic Astrology, from India, is the study and practise of predictive astrology and is the oldest astrological system known to humankind, dating back to before 3000 BCE, remaining almost unchanged since then. As one of the true ancient systems of astrology, Vedic or Hindu Astrology is renowned for its spiritual depth and accuracy in predicting future events, revealing one's destiny and relationship compatibility, as well as many other aspects of Human life.

- Vedic Astrology is known as Jyotish Shastra in Sanskrit and is based on the Vedas, the original scriptures of India and, perhaps, of all Indo-European societies.

- There are nine planets which are considered in Vedic astrology. These are: Mars, Saturn, Jupiter, Mercury, Venus, Sun and Moon (though luminaries are also considered planets), along with Rahu and Ketu (the Dragon's Head and Tail respectively), which are also considered planets.

- At any moment in time, say, at the time of the birth of an individual, the planets are in a definite configuration and can be graphically represented. This configuration is called the horoscope or Birth Chart of the individual. We will refer to this Birth Chart as the "static chart". We call it so because at the time of birth this configuration of the planets is akin to the stamping of a seal which remains with the person for the rest of the life, until death. The configuration of planets that form our static Birth Chart is not in our control and is dictated by our past Karmas.

- Over a long period of experience, it has been found that this configuration of the planets also happens to represent the collective past Karmas of an individual's life, for the reason that during the course of one's life, not all of one's actions give positive results in spite of one being honest, sincere and diligent. On the other hand, despite acting contrary to these virtues, one may get a positive result of one's actions. There seems to be no justification in this, except that it is the result of an innate force, such as latencies of past life Karmas, which decide the outcome of one's present actions.

Bhagavad-Gita: An Astrological Aspect

In the grand scheme of things in Vedic Astrology, the planets play the following roles:

- Saturn: Deemed to be an old, wise man. It represents the masses, the impoverished and collectively become a force to reckon with. In its final forward motion, it becomes so strong that no one can stand before it. It is similar to a judge's role in a court. Saturn is known for giving the fruits of our Karmas – good, bad and mixed.

- Jupiter: It is the helper, the teacher, the benevolent, the son and the brother. It morally binds itself with the 5th and 7th house, and also the 5th with 7th house to construct the 9th house from its position of transit with the help of the 5th and 7th house.

- Sun/Venus/Mercury: They are the executors – directly responsible for executing the plans of Jupiter. They represent the King, Queen and Prime Minister. Mercury executes/manipulates the decisions of the King and Queen because it wants to take advantage of the situation for his personal benefit.

- Mars: It disciplines the house it enters as it is the commander-in-chief. Maintains orderliness.

- Moon: It is the mind of the Sun. The Moon passes on the collective influence of the Sun, Venus and Mercury to the lord of each Nakshatra and to the house where the lord of the Nakshatra is placed in the Birth Chart of the person. This will be referred to as the "Static Chart" or horoscope.

Bhagavad-Gita: An Astrological Aspect

- The Planets Mercury and Venus are never more than 28 degrees and 48 degrees from the Sun. This triad works as one entity and passes on the net influence to the Moon.

- Although the planets have their own traits, yet they do not independently lend their features to an individual. In fact, they all work in tandem to create an individual's personality, and since the configuration of the planets is always changing, no two individuals will ever have the same personality. The actions, reactions and perspective of individuals towards other individuals, places and situations shall vary. We will call these ever-moving planets that are working in tandem in a specific sequence related to one another as "dynamic planets". We will refer to this specific sequence of the planets Mars, Saturn, Jupiter, Ketu & Rahu, Sun, Mercury, Venus and lastly the Moon. They have been discovered to be latently linked to one another as beads in a garland. It is evident from this sequence that the Moon is the final port-of-call for the development of the personality of a person. Since the Moon can occupy any of the 27 Nakshatras of the Zodiac, it further defines the quality of a person. The term Nakshatra is a Sanskrit portmanteau word, formed by joining two words – "naks" meaning the sky and "kshetra" meaning region. Ancient astrologers divided the sky into 27 parts, thereby forming a map of the sky. Each part is considered a lunar mansion because the Moon passes through or resides in each of them for approximately one day. According to Matsya Purana and Padma Purana, Prajapati Daksha, the son of Lord Brahma, married 27 of his daughters to Chandra Deva, and they came to be known as the Moon's Nakshatras.

Bhagavad-Gita: An Astrological Aspect

Predicting Events by the Transit of Planets

After studying various aspects of astrology since the age of 15, Mr Chand Karan Ahuja felt he was stuck with the Dasha system. He was not satisfied with it as it did not yield consistent results. So he conducted his own research to study the science behind the occurrence of events by gochar phal (transit of planets). After many years of research, he discovered irrefutable evidence of the effect of the Zodiac signs during certain specific periods of the year. This research paper was published by the American Federation of Astrologers in their journal in 2014 under the title "Predicting Events". He discovered that an individual is affected by the house of the horoscope whose sign is prevailing at that moment of time as per the chart depicting event/action period of the Zodiac signs as shown in the following table:

Aries	26th July to 20th August
Taurus	21st August to 18th September
Gemini	19th September to 17th October
Cancer	18th October to 12th November
Leo	13th November to 6th December
Virgo	7th December to 31st December
Libra	1st January to 30th January

Scorpio	31st January to 12th March
Sagittarius	13th March to 26th April
Capricorn	27th April to 2nd June
Aquarius	3rd June to 30th June
Pisces	1st July to 25th July

Please note that these periods may begin and end a day or two earlier or later than mentioned. This is because these dates and periods have been calculated with reference to the latitude of New Delhi, India. For cities on other latitudes, these dates may vary by a day or two.

Lord Krishna's Birth Chart: While Krishna is above all astrological aspects, still the Lord followed His own creation of the cycle of birth and death.

There is no accurate data available that provides the exact date and time of Lord Krishna's birth. However, there is a poem by Surdas which eulogized Lord Krishna and described the position of planets at the time of His birth in the following verses:

> Samvat saras vibhavan, Bhado aath tithi budhvaar,
> Krishan paksh Rohini, Ardh nisi harshan jogudaar,
> Vrish hai lagan, ucha ke nisipati, tanhi bahutsukh pe hai,
> Chauthe sinh rasi ke dinkar, jiti sakal ma hi lehey,
> Panchvey budh kanya ko jo hai, putrani bahut bade hai,
> Chatvey shukra tula ke shani jut datru rahan nahipe hai,
> Unch neech yuvati bahu kari hai, satvey rahu pare hai,
> Bhagye bhavan mei maker mahi sut, nahu aishvarya bade hai,
> Laabh bhavan mei meen brihaspati, nav nidhi ghar mei aihey,
> Karam bhavan ke iis, sanichar syam baran tan aihey,
> Audi sanavan parbra ham prabhu, ghat-ghat antarjami,
> Sau turn hare avtarey aani ke, Surdass ke swami.

From these verses we can analyse a few aspects of Lord Krishna's Birth Chart.

Lord Krishna's Birth Chart

- **Rohini Nakshatra:** This is the "star of ascent". The story of the Moon reflects the sufferings which our intense desires may bring, for the Moon could not control his desire for Rohini. This is a passionate Nakshatra and individuals born under this Nakshatra are very attractive, alluring and beautiful. They love luxury, art, music and all the finer things life has to offer. They may come across as materialistic or spoiled as they have very high standards. They can be very artistic and have an appreciation for beauty and the fine arts. This is a growth-oriented Nakshatra, ruling crops and fertility. This implies they can rise to the top and achieve their desires. Also, there is fertility for procreation, meaning they have children.

- **Taurus Ascendant:** Those born under this sign appear to be extremely grounded, steady and stable. The steadying, stable, earthy influence on Taurus rising results in a number of displayed personality traits and a handsome appearance. Those born under this sign have impeccable deportment, disposition and extensive renown.

- **Exalted Moon:** The position of the Moon in the sign of Taurus, especially in the Nakshatra of Rohini, is exalted and lends positive qualities of a good personality and being a humble, loving and handsome individual. The mind is focused and rigid with determination like a bull.

- **Born on Krishna Paksh Ashtami:** This is the concluding day when the previous set of events end and a new set of events begin. The past gets blended into the present and future at this point in time, and therefore this day of the Hindu calendar is considered a very important and crucial day.

Bhagavad-Gita: An Astrological Aspect
The Mahabharata War

- The Mahabharata war, as mentioned in the Bhagavad-Gita, took place in the lunar month of Margshish, i.e., 15 November–15 December, as per the Hindu calendar. The lord of the month of Margshish is Mars, the planet which signifies fighters, warriors, courageous and confident people, full of pride, hasty and quick in action. The war began on the Shukal Paksh (waxing moon) Ekadshi of the lunar month of Margshish, which places the moon in the sign of Aries, which is also represented by Mars. It is most likely that the moon was also transiting through the sign of Aries in the Nakshatra of Ashwini whose ruler is Ketu, which also represents weapons. Being the 6th house from Scorpio, the month of Margshish, indicates opposition and enemies. This brings two warring parties in confrontation with each other as both the Sun and Moon are in the sign of Mars. It took 18 days for this lunar month to come to a conclusion, which was the duration of the Mahabharata war.
- Since the Moon was transiting from the 1st house (Scorpio) towards the 7th house, the period when a person has no free will and has to take action, the occurrence of the war was imminent because during that time Arjuna was unable to exercise his free will; despite being highly reluctant of engaging in the war, he still took part in it.
- The first indications of winning the war came on the 4th day of the war when it was full Moon in Taurus in the Nakshatra of Rohini in the 7th house. Bhishmapitama was wounded grievously on this day. This full Moon marks the first day of success for the sign of Scorpio, which concludes on the day of amavas (no-Moon), thereby making the duration of the war 18 days, i.e., the initial 4 days being the transit of the Moon from the Nakshatra of Ashwini to Rohini (full Moon day) and the next 14 days being the period of full Moon day to no-Moon day/amavas (Taurus to Scorpio).

Lord Krishna said to Arjuna while revealing the Bhagavad-Gita, "Whether I tell you to fight or not, you will fight the war." Arjuna was in a dilemma and reluctant to fight, but Lord Krishna said that even if the other party starts the fight, Arjuna will have to fight to defend, and therefore the occurrence of the war was imminent.

Birth of Bhagavad-Gita:
The Scripture That Comes from the Lord

- The battle was fought in Kurukshetra on the Ekadshi of Shukla Paksha in the Margshirsha month (around November). Ekadshi is the 11th day and Shukla Paksha is when the moon is waxing.

- This is also the time of birth of the most spiritual scriptures, the Bhagavad-Gita, that comes from Lord Krishna. This knowledge had gone missing from this earth as revealed by the Lord Himself in the 4th chapter of the Bhagavad-Gita.

- Ekadshi is a goddess and is the Internal Potency of Lord Narayana. People following Krishna Conscious movement observe fast on every Ekadshi. This event comes twice every month.

- The date and place (Kurukshetra in India) for the most memorable battle was carefully chosen by Lord Krishna.

- By popular tradition, the Kaliyug (Kali Age) started with the death of Lord Krishna, 35 years after the war. Kaliyug began with a grand planetary conjunction.

Blessings by Birth: Astrological Aspect

- Every Birth Chart is different.
- Some charts show the divinity of a person by way of certain configurations of the planets in the chart. This can be studied by examining the association of the ascendant and the lord of the ascendant with the 9th house and the lord of the 9th house. Some charts depict a rich material life and good fortune. Some charts depict a difficult health throughout the life.
- Birth Charts depict almost everything about the Human Being and are the result of the past Karmas of an individual and represent continuity of birth from previous births.

Astrological Aspect

A person performs prescribed or prohibited actions under the influence of latencies of past Karmas – Lord Krishna – BG 18.15.

- This is an important aspect that we perform both prescribed and prohibited actions because of influence of past Karmas.
- The intensity of the influence of the transiting Saturn is at its peak during its last forward motion in the Zodiac sign where it is transiting. It is in this period of the last few months when Saturn begins its forward motion for the last time in that sign, that one reaps the fruits of past Karmas as per the configuration of the planets in an individual's Birth Chart. During the earlier motions of Saturn, whether retrograde or forward in that Zodiac sign, it merely sets out the stage to deliver the fruits in the last period.

Knowledge of the Soul: Astrological Aspect

- We see that there is a continuity of births and Soul, which is a fragment of God that never dies. The Soul takes our mind and senses along when it leaves the body. It then acquires a new body according to our Karmas. This is the reason that every Birth Chart is different because everyone's Karmas are different.
- Our Birth Chart is the sum total of all our previous Karmas and actions performed with our Nature.
- Everything that will happen with us based on our past Karmas is called latencies of past Karmas in Bhagavad-Gita. This is what is there in the Birth Chart.
- God is a True Guide and Witness inside us so He knows every action, every thought that comes to our mind. Anyone watching us does not change our Birth Chart, it is only God watching us that changes our Birth Chart.
- All our past Karmas and resulting actions are handed over by God's system to the Planetary System constituting our Birth Chart or we can say that Execution happens through the Planetary System.
- Our Soul waits for the right configuration of the Planetary System to take place according to our Karmas and then it takes birth.
- Nothing is incidental – everything is minutely planned according to our Nature and Karmas.
- What we do in this birth either through independence of our thoughts or through the influence of the Planetary System adds to our Karmas through this life and makes our next Birth Chart.

End of Mahabharata Was Decided before the War Began

- Karmas had decided the end of the war under the guidance of the Supreme, Sri Krishna.
- Astrological events work as per the laws of Karmas and the Lord had decided the end of the war Himself. He said that "I am the eternal Time spirit". The Lord took charge of everything including the Planetary System which is just a small fragment of His creation and decides everything for us.
- **_Kill Drona and Bhishma and Jaydratha and Karna and other brave warriors, who already stand killed by Me – Lord Krishna to Arjuna – BG 11.34._**

    So end of Mahabharata was already decided by the Lord; Arjuna was tasked with the execution. We can also say that he was chosen for execution because of his good deeds and divine Nature.

Divine or Demoniac Propensities by Birth

Astrological Aspect

In Chapter 16 of the Bhagavad-Gita, Lord Krishna says that people are born with Divine or Demoniac Propensities as there is continuity of the impact of Karmas birth-after-birth. This means that some people have a Divine Birth Chart and some do not have that, which is related to past Karmas.

There are only two types of persons in this world, Arjuna, the one possessing a divine nature and the other possessing a demoniac disposition – Lord Krishna – BG 16.6.

The divine endowment has been recognized as conducive to liberation, and the demoniac one as leading to bondage – Lord Krishna – BG 16.5.

Reactions of Karmas

- The Planetary System executes the results of all our Karmas. The Lord, in His un-manifest form, is a witness to everything that we do. Our Karmas and Nature translate to our Birth Chart. The Planetary System takes over after we are born and works on us till we die. All our Karmas keep adding on to our previous Karmas. Karmas, Nature, likes and dislikes move along with the Soul to the next birth and the Planetary System again takes over from our next Birth Chart. This cycle has been going on for ages and will keep going on for ages and we may never come out of it. But the Bhagavad-Gita guides us on the direction to take to come out of these cycles of birth-and-death.

- The Lord has a system that works on the results, that is why the Lord asks us to just stay focused on righteous Karmas. That system is flawless and it works with precision and accuracy. The results are in the hands of our own Karmas. So the Lord has advised us not to be focused on the outcomes but focus on the right Karmas.

- We are all mounted on a machine. This machine is run by God's Maya, which is the Planetary System and this system works as per our past Karmas and our Nature. **God abides in the heart of all creatures causing them to revolve according to their Karma by His illusive power (Maya) as though mounted on a machine – Lord Krishna – BG 18.61.**

Planetary System: Sun, Moon and the Time of Death

➤ Lord Krishna says – I am the Sun and I am the Moon. The Lord has mentioned many times that He is the Moon and He has also mentioned that He is the mind in Human Beings.

➤ Lord Krishna is also a witness of everything that we do. He is also the Soul that carries our Karmas, mind, and intelligence to the next birth. The Planetary System that does all the execution is also His creation.

Arjuna – I shall now tell you the time (path) departing when Yogis do not return, and also the time (path) departing when they do return – Lord Krishna – BG 8.23.

(Of the two paths), the one in which are stationed the all-effulgent fire-god and the deities presiding over daylight, the bright fortnight, and the six months of the northward course of the Sun respectively; proceeding along it after death Yogis, who have known Brahma, being successively led by the above gods, finally reach Brahma – Lord Krishna – BG 8.24.

The other path is that wherein are stationed the gods presiding over smoke, night, the dark fortnight, and the six months of the southward course of the Sun; the Yogi (devoted to action with an interested motive) taking to this path after death is led by these gods, one after another, and attaining the lustre of Moon (and enjoying the fruit of his meritorious deeds in Heaven) returns to this mortal world – Lord Krishna – BG 8.25.

Among sacrifices, I am the sacrifice of japa (intonation of sacred chants) – Lord Krishna – BG 10.25.

Sacrifice or doing japa is linked to the spiritual aspect in one's life. Sacrifice is an inherent characteristic of spirituality, and is reflected in the horoscope of an individual, as per the configuration of the planets at the time of birth.

Cosmic Day and Cosmic Night

- The Planetary System started with the start of the creation of this universe and it will end its life with the end of this universe.
- When all the powers of this universe are extinguished, it is called the night of Lord Brahma. All Souls merge into the subtle body of Lord Brahma. Day is of same duration as night. At the start of the next day, a new Planetary System gets created and this cycle goes on. It has been there for ever and it will be there for ever. All Souls re-appear at the start of the day according the Karmas of their previous births.
- While we all get influenced so severely by the Planetary System which is the result of our own Karmas, we must work to look at the science behind astrology, which is so well explained by Lord Krishna in the Bhagavad-Gita. This is the opportunity for us to defeat this system and get above this system.
- Even when the Final Dissolution takes place, our Karmas still stay with us and when we are reborn, we are again reborn according to our Karmas. Our Karmas do not leave us. So we need to be cautious.
- This means that our first Birth Chart is also based on our latencies of past births. The Planetary System starts working on us from the start.
- In the Bhagavad-Gita, Shri Krishna reveals how to come out of this never-ending cycle in which we have got ourselves caught due to our own actions.

Three Gunas

- The Planetary System represents the three Gunas and everyone Below Time is influenced by the three Gunas. No god is free from these three Gunas if the god's existence is Below Time. All universes are Below Time. This is the Maya that keeps us within the universe and birth after birth; we just continue here in some body or the other, depending on our Karmas.
- Lord Krishna says that His Maya is extremely difficult to break through, but worshippers or devotees of the Lord are able to break through.

There is no being on earth, or in the middle region or even among the gods or anywhere else, who is free from these three Gunas born of Prakriti – Lord Krishna – BG 18.40.

CHAPTER 18
Key Verses in Bhagavad-Gita with Deep Messages

Battle of Mahabharata: Advice of Lord Krishna to Arjuna

अशोच्यानन्वशोचस्त्वं प्रज्ञावादांश्च भाषसे |
गतासूनगतासूंश्च नानुशोचन्ति पण्डिताः ||

You grieve over those who should not be grieved for and yet speak like the learned; wise men do not sorrow over the dead or the living – Lord Krishna – BG 2.11.

The Mahabharata is the only battle where Lord Krishna Himself was present, though He did not fight. This historic battle between cousin brothers, relatives and friends saw a huge loss of human lives. People with extraordinary spiritual blessings and skills took the side of wrong-doers. While many of them were worthy of being respected and even worshipped, for their own reasons due to past event, they took the side of wrong, not knowing what was in store in future.

Lord Krishna says to Arjuna – The brilliant, pious and the extraordinary taking the side of wrongdoers are not worth grieving for and need to lose their lives since the Lord was present to see that righteousness was established back on mother earth.

Science of the Soul: Imperishable and Personal Identity

अच्छेद्योऽयमदाह्योऽयमक्लेद्योऽशोष्य एव च |
नित्य: सर्वगत: स्थाणुरचलोऽयं सनातन: ||

This Soul is incapable of being cut, or burnt by fire; nor can it be dissolved by water and cannot be dried by air either. This Soul is eternal, all-pervading, immovable, constant and everlasting – Lord Krishna – BG 2.24.

The Soul is God's fragment in us, in everyone – Human Beings, animals and other types of existences. This Soul is personal to us and moves with us from one birth to the next to the next. Whether we migrate to higher abodes or animal lives, same Soul remains with us. This is the consciousness in us and we are alive because of this. This is not part of the 5 Tattvas that we know from which every material thing is made – earth, water, fire, air and ether. This Soul never dies. It does not belong to this universe which is perishable. Even when everything dies, this Soul will remain and will migrate Above Time.

The Soul is eternal – it was always there even before this universe was formed. It is all-pervading and can migrate to any region. It is constant and does not go high or low or up or down. The Soul in us carries all our Karmas and Nature to the next birth and decides the next type of birth. The Soul is always connected with Oversoul which is Krishna, because it is His fragment and it abides in the heart.

Science of the Soul: Un-manifest and Immutable

अव्यक्तोऽयमचिन्त्योऽयमविकार्योऽयमुच्यते |
तस्मादेवं विदित्वैनं नानुशोचितुमर्हसि ||

This Soul is un-manifest, it is incomprehensible, and it is spoken of us immutable – Lord Krishna – BG 2.25.

Lord Krishna further explains the Nature of this Soul which is a fragment of the Lord or the Oversoul. This Soul cannot be seen as it is un-manifest. This means that we, who are living in this material world, cannot see the Soul. It does not belong to this world. It has migrated here from the Lord's Abode perhaps because we wanted to experiment. This Soul has the record of all our previous births and what we have done so far. When it migrates from one body to the next, it carries all these. The Soul does not get impure if it is in an impious Human Being or an animal or any other living being; it just carries on it the burden of our Nature and Karmas.

This Soul cannot be muted like we mute material things. Even the most spiritual people cannot mute it because the Soul is the Lord Himself.

Science of the Soul: Only a Worthy One Knows about It

आश्चर्यवत्पश्यति कश्चिदेन माश्चर्यवद्वदति तथैव चान्यः |
आश्चर्यवच्चैनमन्यः शृणोति श्रुत्वाप्येनं वेद न चैव कश्चित् ||

Hardly any great Soul perceives this Soul as marvellous, scarce another great Soul likewise speaks thereof as marvellous, and scarce another worthy one hears of it as marvellous, while there are some who know it not even on hearing of it – Lord Krishna – BG 2.29.

Spiritual knowledge and advancement is a journey. We cannot bypass or advance it by avoiding going through the path. Committed persons can complete the journey to Lord's Abode within this birth. Understanding the Soul and role of the Soul is fundamental to the advancement on the spiritual path. Understanding that there is a Lord and that the Lord is fully present in us is the key spiritual learning.

Lord Krishna says that a well deserving person on this path understands about this; there is a rare person who explains about this; and only a worthy one whose Karmas (past and present) support him to listen, understand and appreciate this marvellous subject. There are many persons who do get the opportunity to hear about this but do not pay any attention because they are not on the path to the spiritual journey.

Righteous War or Unsolicited War: We Must Do Our Duty

अथ चेत्त्वमिमं धर्म्यं संग्रामं न करिष्यसि ।
ततः स्वधर्मं कीर्तिं च हित्वा पापमवाप्स्यसि ॥

Arjuna, if you refuse to fight this righteous war then, shirking your duty and losing your reputation, you will incur sin –- Lord Krishna – BG 2.33.

Mahabharata was an un-solicited war. Lord Krishna had already explained to Arjuna that all attempts to avoid the war had failed. At the same time, unrighteousness was increasing for which the Lord had appeared on the earth.

Arjuna was Kshatriya (warrior) by birth and by Nature. So it was his duty to fight this war to help God's system to eradicate the sinful people, whose numbers had grown. Every person has to perform his duties. That is why the Lord told Arjuna that he must fight this righteous war, otherwise he would incur sin because he had been chosen by God to perform the task based on the merits of his Nature and past Karmas. While the end of the war was already decided by God, we all have to play our roles, so the Lord is advising Arjuna to play his role.

Karmayoga Leads to Liberation

नेहाभिक्रमनाशोऽस्ति प्रत्यवायो न विद्यते ।
स्वल्पमप्यस्य धर्मस्य त्रायते महतो भयात् ॥

In this path (of selfless action) there is no loss of effort, nor is there fear of contrary result; even a little practise of this discipline saves one from the terrible fear of birth and death – Lord Krishna – BG 2.40.

Here the Lord sows the seeds of enlightenment and liberation in Arjuna. The Lord explains about Karmayoga, which is about doing the right thing, not being worried about the outcome, not planning the result but performing the duties as a surrender to God. The Lord says that when you perform the duties with surrender in mind, then there is no contrary result – even if you lose the war, you have done your righteous duty. The Lord had already explained to Arjuna that even if he lost the war and was killed, he would still go to God's Abode.

Now the Lord explains this further and says that that if a person performs the actions as explained, he will be saved from the terrible fear of birth and death, which means that this will take the person to the Lord's Abode Above Time and the person will not need to go through the cycles of birth and death.

Enlightenment Is to Live in God's Thoughts Above Time

यावानर्थ उदपाने सर्वतः सम्प्लुतोदके |
तावान्सर्वेषु वेदेषु ब्राह्मणस्य विजानतः ||

A Brahmana who has obtained enlightenment, has as much use for all the Vedas as one who, standing on the brink of a sheet of water overflowing on all sides, has for a small reservoir of water – Lord Krishna – BG 2.46.

There are two existences – the first is Below Time, which is our universe that consists of 14 worlds out of which earth is one and is in the middle. The second existence is Above Time, where nothing changes with time because it is Above Time. Worlds Below Time are material worlds and worlds Above Time are spiritual worlds. God's Abode is Above Time.

Vedas were given by God when the universe was created and hence the Vedas have all the knowledge for every problem related to this and all other universes. The other important knowledge in the Vedas is about uniting the Soul with the Lord. An enlightened person, though living in the material world, does not believe that he belongs to the material world and so nothing attracts him as he is spiritually connected with God, who is Above Time. Since the enlightened person knows that everything in this material world is temporary, he is neither attracted nor makes any attempt to fulfil his material wishes. So even the Vedas, which describe means to attain worldly desires, do not mean anything to him.

The enlightened person is absorbed in God Above Time, who is overflowing with nectar all the time and he enjoys that nectar which is for ever and will continue after his death also. The Vedas have served the purpose of uniting him with the Almighty and now he is in the state of liberation while living in this body.

God's System Is Working as per Our Karmas; We Need Not Interfere

कर्मण्येवाधिकारस्ते मा फलेषु कदाचन ।
मा कर्मफलहेतुर्भूर्मा ते सङ्गोऽस्त्वकर्मणि ॥

Your right is to work only and never to the fruit thereof. Do not consider yourself to be the cause of the fruit of action; nor let your attachment be to inaction – Lord Krishna – BG 2.47.

Lord Krishna advises Arjuna to focus on his righteous Karmas only. He should not focus on the results. God's system is working on the right results so he does not need to worry or interfere in God's planning or God's system. That system is very accurate. The system takes decisions based on Karmas of all births. The system will anyway overrule the individual's planning. So it is short-sighted to become the cause and all the personal effort in this manner will create material bonds, whereas the Bhagavad-Gita is about liberation.

As an example, the end of Mahabharata war was already decided before the war started. Arjuna was chosen to be an instrument of God's will by God Himself. Arjuna's merits enabled him to get selected as the principle warrior. If he fought based on his ego, then he would be bound by his actions but if he fought in the true spirit of Karmayoga with complete surrender to the Lord, he would be liberated.

The Lord also cautioned that this thought should not result in people deciding not to act. Performing one's duties is a must.

Spirit of Sacrifice Takes You to God's Abode

यज्ञार्थात्कर्मणोऽन्यत्र लोकोऽयं कर्मबन्धनः ।
तदर्थं कर्म कौन्तेय मुक्तसङ्गः समाचर ॥
यज्ञशिष्टाशिनःसन्तो मुच्यन्ते सर्वकिल्बिषैः ।
भुञ्जते ते त्वघं पापा ये पचन्त्यात्मकारणात् ॥

Man is bound by his own actions except when they are performed for the sake of sacrifice. Therefore, Arjuna, perform your duty efficiently, free from attachment, for the sake of sacrifice alone. The virtuous who partake of what is left over after sacrifice, are absolved of all sins. Those sinful ones who cook for the sake of nourishing their bodies alone, partake of sin only – Lord Krishna – BG 3.9 and 3.13.

The difference between action and sacrifice is that actions (that bind us) are the ones that are performed for our self-pleasure or ego. Sacrifice are the actions that are performed for others, in a spirit of service to the Lord – that everything belongs to the Lord and we are just doing our duties in His creation. Anything that is performed for others – family, society, service to Lord – is sacrifice and is sattvik.

Sacrifice removes all our sins. Sacrifice means that we are working in the spirit that everything belongs to God. Sacrifice does not bind us to this material world. Every act of sacrifice takes us closer to God and when practised naturally over our life, it enables us to reach the Lord's Abode.

All-Pervading Infinite Is Always Present in Sacrifice

तस्मात्सर्वगतं ब्रह्म नित्यं यज्ञे प्रतिष्ठितम् ।

All pervading Infinite is always present in Sacrifice – Lord Krishna – BG 3.15.

All pervading Infinite is worshipped as OM. OM is Krishna's un-manifest form which is present everywhere – within us, outside us, in everything, in all the universes. Nothing can exist without un-manifest God. Everything is threaded on Him.

He is the sound that resonates between all the universes, in ether, in air and everywhere. Since the un-manifest form is spiritual, our material form is unable to see it, but enlightened people can realize Him. He has hands and feet everywhere, He has His face on all sides as He pervades the universe. He is best addressed as OM–TAT–SAT and His Nature is Truth–Consciousness–Bliss. He is present everywhere and is the only truth; we and other existences are perishable, only He is the truth. He is conscious and is listening and guiding all of us and He is always blessing.

This Lord is always present in sacrifice so sacrifice is Lord. That is how a person who lives in sacrifice is living in God and his destination is also the Lord.

Bhagavad-Gita Came from Krishna; It Cannot Be Found in Other Scriptures

इमं विवस्वते योगं प्रोक्तवानहमव्ययम् ।
विवस्वान्मनवे प्राह मनुरिक्ष्वाकवेऽब्रवीत् ॥
एवं परम्पराप्राप्तमिमं राजर्षयो विदुः ।
स कालेनेह महता योगो नष्टः परन्तप ॥
स एवायं मया तेऽद्य योगः प्रोक्तः पुरातनः ।
भक्तोऽसि मे सखा चेति रहस्यं ह्येतदुत्तमम् ॥

I revealed this immortal Yoga to Vivasvan (Sun-god); Vivasvan conveyed it to Manu (his son); and Manu imparted it to (his son) Iksvaku. This transmitted in succession from father to son. Arjuna, this Yoga remained known to the Rajarsis (royal sages). Through long lapse of time, this Yoga got lost to the world. The same ancient Yoga, which is the supreme secret, has this day been imparted to you by Me, because you are My devotee and friend – Lord Krishna – BG 4.1–4.3.

Lord Krishna revealed this knowledge to the Sun-god when this universe was born. Then the knowledge went to Manu, who started the Manvantara and the start of Yugas. Then the knowledge went to his son who was the king. But over time this knowledge got lost. Lord Krishna has now revealed the same knowledge to Arjuna. Hence we know that this knowledge cannot be found in any other scripture.

This knowledge is helpful to those who have embarked on the spiritual journey and are devotees of the Supreme Lord.

Lord Manifests on Earth from Time to Time with a Purpose

यदा यदा हि धर्मस्य ग्लानिर्भवति भारत |
अभ्युत्थानमधर्मस्य तदात्मानं सृजाम्यहम् ||
परित्राणाय साधूनां विनाशाय च दुष्कृताम् |
धर्मसंस्थापनार्थाय सम्भवामि युगे युगे ||

Whenever there is a decline in righteousness and an increase in unrighteousness, O Arjuna, at that time I manifest myself on earth. To protect the righteous, to annihilate the wicked, and to re-establish the principles of dharma I appear on this earth, age after age – Lord Krishna – BG 4.7–4.8.

God is present all around us as well as inside us all the time in His un-manifest form. Nothing can exist without Him. He is not realized by all in this form and only people who have spiritually progressed can feel His presence. Also, in the un-manifest form, the Lord's Nature is to bless everyone. Our Karmas are recorded by our Soul and un-manifest form of God; the Planetary System executes the destinies based on that. With time, some evil forces grow so powerful that even the planetary system cannot handle them.

God manifests Himself to establish the righteousness on mother earth. He eradicates the evil doers, some of whom have crossed the limits and become more powerful than the system. God is an example of Karmas and devotion. He uplifts the common person who has not realized the presence of the un-manifest. The presence of the Lord is so pious that everyone who hears and chants His name gets uplifted on the spiritual platform. The Lord becomes an example for us to follow. His activities and childhood stories grow everyone spiritually. So the Lord has to manifest after some interval of time to do good to His creation.

Devotees Look for God, God Looks for Devotees

ये यथा मां प्रपद्यन्ते तांस्तथैव भजाम्यहम् |
मम वर्त्मानुवर्तन्ते मनुष्याः पार्थ सर्वशः ||

Arjuna, howsoever men seek Me, even so do I respond to them; for all men follow My path in every way – Lord Krishna – BG 4.11.

When we worship the Lord with a material desire, then the Lord responds to us by looking after our material desire. This appears as if we are trading with the Lord. When someone worships the Lord with love, the Lord reciprocates with love, which is "Above All".

Meera Bai worshipped Lord Krishna with love, with no material desires and she got Krishna Himself as she had no other desire. The gopis worshipped mother Katyayani with a wish to get Krishna. The Lord is listening to our hearts as He is sitting in our hearts.

There are two existences – spiritual existence and material existence. Spiritual existence is Above Time and is God's Abode. This universe is material existence; it is Below Time and perishable. The highest form of devotion is that, while we have fallen to this material existence, we can stay in love with God in His spiritual existence and away from material desires. If that happens, all our sins will get wiped out as our next destination will be God's Abode which is Above Time and material desires have no presence there. If we stay with material requirements, then we will be reborn in the material world as per our desires, which get fulfilled only as per our Karmas.

Sacrifice: Pleasure of Being Good – Way to God

यज्ञशिष्टामृतभुजो यान्ति ब्रह्म सनातनम् |
नायं लोकोऽस्त्ययज्ञस्य कुतोऽन्य: कुरुसत्तम ||

Arjuna, Yogis who enjoy the nectar that has been left over after the performance of a sacrifice attain the eternal Brahma. To the man who does not offer sacrifice, even this world is not happy; how, then, can the other world be happy? – Lord Krishna – BG 4.31.

Lord Krishna explains the spirit of sacrifice. Everything that we do for the Lord and for His existence in a sattvik form is sacrifice – the food we offer, the words we speak, our deeds and so on. If we adopt sacrifice in every thought and in every act, then this will become our Nature. This Nature will take us to Brahma.

Here the reference to Brahma is OM, which is the un-manifest form of Lord Krishna. People attain Brahma means they migrate to Hari Dham which is Krishna's Abode, Above Time. Everywhere this is referenced. However, there is one more abode – Golok Dham, which is personal to Krishna and Radha. Here reside the devotees and gopis who just want to serve Krishna. The light of OM emerges from Radha and Krishna and travels down to Hari Dham and Shiva Dham (Above Time) and then travels down to all the universe (Below Time).

The Lord also says that those who just work for their own selfish needs get badly caught by Maya and revolve in this universe that has 8.4 million types of species (Human births are 400,000 types as every Human is different, while all other births have similarity in their Nature). People without sacrifice can never be happy; they only imagine they are happy out of ignorance.

Reach God's Abode within This Birth

योगयुक्तो मुनिर्ब्रह्म नचिरेणाधिगच्छति ||

The Karmayogi who keeps his mind fixed on God, reaches Brahma in no time – Lord Krishna – BG 5.6.

There are two types of existences as we saw. One is transcendental (Above Time) which is God's Abode and where there is no pain of birth, death, old age or disease. This is the spiritual world that has no affect from the material world. The other is this material world in which we live (Below Time). This has the inherent pains of birth, death, old age and disease. This world also has presence of spiritual energy that travels down from the spiritual world to the material world.

If we stay connected and absorbed with Brahma (un-manifest) and Krishna (manifest) forms and keep doing all our duties in the material world (which is also a creation of the Lord) in the spirit of Karmayoga (which is offering all our Karmas to the Lord and staying sattvik), then we will reach Brahma (which is Krishna's Abode) immediately after this birth because we are anyway living there in our thoughts all the time and performing deeds for His sake.

Realization of God's Presence All Around Us

कामक्रोधवियुक्तानां यतीनां यतचेतसाम् |
अभितो ब्रह्मनिर्वाणं वर्तते विदितात्मनाम् ||

To those wise men who are free from lust and anger, who have subdued their mind and have realized God, Brahma, the abode of eternal peace, is present all around – Lord Krishna – BG 5.26.

Lord Krishna, in the form of OM, is present all around us. There is nothing that can exist without this energy and un-manifest God. Then what is the reason that we do not realize His presence? It is our anger, ego, desire and greed that keeps us awake in the material world by the force of Maya. We stay engaged in its activities and reactions and have gone through million of births in various types and forms.

However, if we now turn inwards and stop getting influenced by lust, anger and the happenings around, then we will feel the presence of Lord. That will bring us extreme peace and happiness, which is the real sattvik happiness. The happiness that we know in the material world is Rajasic or Tamasic happiness.

When we rise above the material attractions and repulsions and realize the real peace, then we have realized Brahma. Then God's Abode becomes our real destination when we complete this birth.

Spiritual Aspirants Reach God in This Birth or Next

पार्थ नैवेह नामुत्र विनाशस्तस्य विद्यते ।
न हि कल्याणकृत्कश्चिद्दुर्गतिं तात गच्छति ॥
प्राप्य पुण्यकृतां लोकानुषित्वा शाश्वती: समा: ।
शुचीनां श्रीमतां गेहे योगभ्रष्टोऽभिजायते ॥
पूर्वाभ्यासेन तेनैव ह्रियते ह्यवशोऽपि स: ।
जिज्ञासुरपि योगस्य शब्दब्रह्मातिवर्तते ॥

There is no fall for one who strives for self-redemption. None ever meets with evil destiny. Such a person who has strayed from Yoga, obtains the higher worlds (Heaven etc.) to which men of meritorious deeds alone are entitled, and having resided there for innumerable years, take birth of pious and prosperous parents. They continue the spiritual journey from the previous birth and are more committed – Lord Krishna – BG 6.40, 6.41, 6.44.

Spiritual aspirants are protected by God and God's system and continue making progress towards God's Abode till they reach there. If they fail to reach in one birth then they make it in the next. There are two types of failed aspirants.

The first type of spiritual aspirants who could not reach God's Abode in one birth:

These aspirants had some desires and they needed to fulfil them. They travel to Heavenly Abodes, fulfil their desires and then take birth in rich and pious families. They inherit the spirit of the spiritual journey and work harder to reach God's Abode in that birth.

Spiritual Aspirants Reach God in This Birth or Next

अथवा योगिनामेव कुले भवति धीमताम् ।
एतद्धि दुर्लभतरं लोके जन्म यदीदृशम् ॥
तत्र तं बुद्धिसंयोगं लभते पौर्वदेहिकम् ।
यतते च ततो भूयः संसिद्धौ कुरुनन्दन ॥

If he is possessed of dispassion, then not attaining those regions he is born in the family of enlightened Yogis; but such a birth in this world is very difficult to obtain. He automatically regains in that birth the latencies of even-mindedness of his previous birth; and through that he strives harder than ever for perfection in the form of God-realization – Lord Krishna – BG 6.42–6.43.

The second type of spiritual aspirants who could not reach God's Abode in one birth:

These aspirants did not have any desires and were in dispassion. They do not need to go to Heavenly Abodes as that is the place for fulfilling desires. They are immediately reborn in the family of enlightened Yogis but Lord Krishna says that such a birth is very rare. These people go faster to God's Abode as they skip the journey to Heavenly Abodes because they were more committed and loving towards the Lord.

Committed Yogi Reaches God in One Birth with Help from Latencies of Past Karmas

प्रयत्नाद्यतमानस्तु योगी संशुद्धकिल्बिष: |
अनेकजन्मसंसिद्धस्ततो याति परां गतिम् ||

The Yogi, however, who diligently takes up the practice, attains perfection in this very life with the help of latencies of many births, and being thoroughly purged of sin, forthwith reaches the supreme state – Lord Krishna – BG 6.45.

Lord Krishna says that the spiritual aspirant who is committed to reach God can make it in this very birth itself. We face obstacles of family, society, environment and reactions of past Karmas that distract us or slow down our journey towards God's Abode. But for a committed Yogi, latencies of good Karmas of the past amplify and remove the obstacles and with God's blessings, he reaches God's Abode in this very birth.

Yogi Is Superior to Ascetics

तपस्विभ्योऽधिकोयोगी ज्ञानिभ्योऽपिमतोऽधिकः।
कर्मिभ्यश्चाधिकोयोगी तस्माद्योगीभवार्जुन॥

The Yogi is superior to ascetics; he is regarded superior even to those versed in sacred lore. The Yogi is also superior to those who perform action with some interested motive. Therefore, Arjuna, do become a Yogi – Lord Krishna – BG 6.46.

Lord Krishna says that a Karmayogi who is focused on performing all his duties in a sattvik manner and offers everything to the Lord is superior to ascetics. Lord Krishna has revealed that Karmayogis reach the same destination as those in Karma sanyasa, but performing Karmas is an easier and faster path to reach God's Abode.

Krishna's Un-manifest Form Pervades All the Universes

रसोऽहमप्सु कौन्तेय प्रभास्मि शशिसूर्ययोः ।
प्रणवः सर्ववेदेषु शब्दः खे पौरुषं नृषु ॥
पुण्यो गन्धः पृथिव्यां च तेजश्चास्मि विभावसौ ।
जीवनं सर्वभूतेषु तपश्चास्मि तपस्विषु ॥
बीजं मां सर्वभूतानां विद्धि पार्थ सनातनम् ।
बुद्धिर्बुद्धिमतामस्मि तेजस्तेजस्विनामहम् ॥
बहूनां जन्मनामन्ते ज्ञानवान्मां प्रपद्यते ।
वासुदेवः सर्वमिति स महात्मा सुदुर्लभः ॥

I am sapidity in water and the radiance in the Moon and the Sun; I am the sacred syllable OM in all the Vedas, the sound in ether and virility in men. I am life in all beings and austerity in ascetics. I am the eternal seed of all beings. In the very last of all births the enlightened person worships Me by realizing that all this is God. Such a Soul is very rare indeed – Lord Krishna – BG 7.8–7.10, 7.19.

There is nothing that can exist without Lord Krishna. Everything is Krishna. We have Krishna inside and we have Krishna outside. He exists within us in our heart. He exists without us – in the sound in the vacuum, in living and non-living beings. He is the radiance in the Sun. His energy nourishes all the plants and fruits.

Realizing this and continuing in the spiritual journey, a person finally reaches a birth where he realizes this truth. He feels Lord's presence all around. That is the last birth of the Human Being before he migrates to the Supreme Abode.

Krishna Is Sitting Inside Us and Is Witness to Whatever We Do

अक्षरं ब्रह्म परमं स्वभावोऽध्यात्ममुच्यते ||
अधिभूतं क्षरो भावः पुरुषश्चाधिदैवतम् |
अधियज्ञोऽहमेवात्र देहे देहभृतां वर ||

The supreme indestructible is Brahman. One's own Self (the individual Soul), is called Adhyatama. All perishable objects are Adhibhuta; the shining Purusha (Brahma) is Adhidaiva; and in this body I Myself, dwelling as the inner witness, am Adhiyajna – Lord Krishna – BG 8.3–8.4.

Lord Krishna explains the various entities:

1. There is one un-manifest God. He is known as OM. He is also known as Brahman. He has hands and feet all over, a face in all directions and is pervading this universe and between the universes.

2. The Lord is present in each one of us. Based on our Karmas, our individual Soul migrates to different births. This identity that is associated with every individual is called Adhyatama.

3. Everything on this earth will perish except our Souls. These perishable things in this universe are called Adhibhuta.

4. Lord Brahma created this universe and will run this universe for a hundred years. In one day of Lord Brahma, we probably take million births and still we never get out of this existence Below Time. The creator of this universe has been addressed by Lord Krishna as Adhidaiva – the shining Purusha.

5. The Soul inside us is a fragment of Lord Krishna. He is our consciousness. He is guide, mentor, father, friend, but at the same time, He is also witness to whatever we do. His form to monitor our Karmas is called Adhiyajna.

Principle of Karmayoga: Way to God's Abode

तस्मात्सर्वेषु कालेषु मामनुस्मर युध्य च |
मय्यर्पितमनोबुद्धिर्मामेवैष्यस्यसंशयम् ||

Think of Me all times and fight. With mind and reason thus set on Me, you will doubtless come to Me – Lord Krishna – BG 8.7.

This verse has a very deep message, and we can say that this is the "Bhagavad-Gita". Lord Krishna tells Arjuns to do two things – Remember Him all the time and also to fight which is natural duty of the warrior and Lord is advising him to fight only the righteous war. He cannot do only one of these. If he remembers the Lord all the time but does not fight, then he is not doing his duty. If he fights but does not remember Him, then he is bound by his Karmas – even when he wins the battle, he will become the king of the universe and then after death he will be the king of the Heavenly Planets and then he will be born as a king, but he will miss reaching Lord Krishna.

If he remembers the Lord all the time, he will not be affected by the results of his Karmas (good and bad) and his destination will be Lord Krishna. We have to learn and practise to remember the Lord all the time. After some time it will become natural with us and then everything will be so easy and so beautiful.

All Universes Including the One of Creator Brahma Are Below Time

आब्रह्मभुवनाल्लोकाः पुनरावर्तिनोऽर्जुन |
मामुपेत्य तु कौन्तेय पुनर्जन्म न विद्यते ||

Arjuna, all the worlds from Brahmaloka (the heavenly realm of the creator Brahma) downwards are liable to birth and rebirth. But O son of Kunti, on attaining Me there is no rebirth (for, while I am beyond Time, regions like Brahmaloka, being conditioned by Time, are transitory) – Lord Krishna – BG 8.16.

There are 14 worlds in our universe. The earth is in the middle. The worlds above the earth are called Heavenly Planets. The highest of all the planets or abodes is Lord Brahma's abode. Lord Brahma is the creator of this universe (different from Brahman which is OM and Un-manifest Divinity). Mother Ganga lives in Brahma's world also. All existences including Brahma's world are Below Time and hence are under the influence of Maya because all material worlds are impacted by Maya. All gods and demigods within this universe are also influenced by Maya.

Above Time are Shiva Dham, Hari Dham and Golok. These are spiritual worlds and go through no pains that are associated with the material worlds. Once a Soul crosses this timeline, it becomes free from the influence of Maya. Once the Soul reaches the spiritual world, it can come down to the material world on it's own wish and is not impacted by the material world.

All worlds including Brahma's lok will get destroyed at some time because these are Below Time.

Brahma's One Day and Our Number of Cycles of Birth and Death

सहस्रयुगपर्यन्तमहर्यद्ब्रह्मणो विदुः |
रात्रिं युगसहस्रान्तां तेऽहोरात्रविदो जनाः ||
अव्यक्ताद्व्यक्तयः सर्वाः प्रभवन्त्यहरागमे |
रात्र्यागमे प्रलीयन्ते तत्रैवाव्यक्तसञ्ज्ञके ||

Those Yogis who know from realization about Brahma's day as covering a thousand Mahayugas, and so his night as extending to another thousand Mahayugas, know the reality about Time. All embodied beings emanate from the Un-manifest (i.e., Brahma's subtle body) at the coming of the cosmic day; at the cosmic nightfall they merge into the same subtle body of Brahma, known as the Un-manifest – Lord Krishna – BG 8.17–8.18.

Lord Brahma, the creator of this universe has a life of 100 years. At the start of the day, the universe is created and at night, everything collapses. All Souls emerge from the subtle body of the creator (Lord Brahma) at the start of the day and merge into him at night. This is called Cosmic Day and Cosmic Night. The life of the Sun, Moon, Earth and others in the planetary system, including heavenly planets and hellish planets, is Brahma's one day. This one day lasts for approximately 4.32 billion years of ours. During this one day we go through millions of births depending on our Karmas and keep running between various existences.

Lord Krishna says that this day is equal to thousand Mahyugas. This means that we go through the cycle of Satyug, Tretayug, Dwaparyug and Kaliyug one thousand times in one Brahma day. But we are still not able to cross the timeline. In the night, all the Souls stay in Brahma's subtle body. Lord Brahma is always Un-manifest.

How important it is for us to walk on path of the Bhagavad-Gita, become free from the universe and cross the timeline!

Revolving in the Same Universe for Millions of Births

भूतग्रामः स एवायं भूत्वा भूत्वा प्रलीयते |
रात्र्यागमेऽवशः पार्थ प्रभवत्यहरागमे ||

This multitude of beings, being born again and again, is dissolved under compulsion of its Nature at the coming of the cosmic night and rises again at the commencement of the cosmic day – Lord Krishna – BG 8.19.

This cycle of day and night (each day and night of 4.32 billion years each) continues for 100 years and we stay within the Brahma Lok which is the abode of creator of the universe (Lord Brahma) and perishes after 100 years.

This is a big realization that we have been here for trillions of years and Lord Krishna is guiding us on a beautiful path that can take us out of this universe to God's Abode within this birth itself (remember, Human birth is not easy to get).

Spiritual World Is Above the Material Worlds

परस्तस्मात्तु भावोऽन्योऽव्यक्तोऽव्यक्तात्सनातन: ।
य: स सर्वेषु भूतेषु नश्यत्सु न विनश्यति ॥
अव्यक्तोऽक्षर इत्युक्तस्तमाहु: परमां गतिम् ।
यं प्राप्य न निवर्तन्ते तद्धाम परमं मम ॥

Far beyond even this Un-manifest, there is yet another Un-manifest Existence, that Supreme Divine Person, who does not Perish even though all beings perish. The same Un-manifest which has been spoken of as the Indestructible, is also called the supreme Goal; that again is MY supreme Abode; attaining which they return not to this mortal world – Lord Krishna – BG 8.20–8.21.

Here Lord Krishna is explaining the difference between the material world (Below Time) and the spiritual world (Above Time). When we say Below Time, we mean there is a life, and there is birth and death. When we say Above Time, we mean there is no cycle of birth and death because the existence is not measured by time. Life span means measurement against time and if there is no time, there is no measurement by time. Up to Brahma Lok, everyone is Below Time. The Lord says that existences above this never get destroyed and are always existing. This is called the Indestructible Brahman and is the Supreme Abode of Lord Krishna. There are distinct existences Above Time – Shiva Dham, Hari Dham, Devi Dham, Saket Dham of Lord Ram and Golok Dham. Lord Narayan or Mahavishnu, from whom all the expansions happen, resides in Hari Dham. Lord Narayan is the first form that Krishna took. Golok Dham is above all and is the personal abode of Lord Krishna and His devotees. All these Dhams are Lord Krishna's spiritual presence in one of the forms.

Krishna, Also Known as Govinda, Is the Reason behind All Reasons

पुरुषः स परः पार्थ भक्त्या लभ्यस्त्वनन्यया |
यस्यान्तःस्थानि भूतानि येन सर्वमिदं ततम् ||

That eternal un-manifest supreme Purusha in whom all beings reside and by whom all this is pervaded, is attainable only through exclusive devotion – Lord Krishna – BG 8.22.

In Brahma Samhita, the first verse is:

ईश्वरः परमः कृष्णः सच्चिदानंद विग्रहः | अनादिरादिर्गोविंदः सर्वकारणकारणम् ||

Lord Govinda is the God whose complete incarnation is only Krishna. He is the reason behind all reasons and there is nothing behind Him. He is the form of OM, or we can say OM emerges from Lord Krishna.

His key forms closest to Him are Narayan in Hari Dham. His Spiritual Potency is Yogamaya. His other closest form close to His attributes is that of Ram. All Dhams, e.g., Shiva Dham, Hari Dham, Ram Dham, Devi Dham and Golok Dham are Above Time so complete devotion of all these Lords can take us Above Time. They are also forms of Krishna as we move to different Dhams in the spiritual world. All expansions have come from Govinda or Krishna or Radha–Krishna. OM and Yogamaya do all the expansions in the spiritual worlds and then in the material world and also sustain everyone.

Knowledge Is Complete When We Know Both Manifest and Un-manifest

राजविद्या राजगुह्यं पवित्रमिदमुत्तमम् |
प्रत्यक्षावगमं धर्म्यं सुसुखं कर्तुमव्ययम् ||

Knowledge of Nirguana and Saguna aspects of Divinity is a sovereign science, a sovereign secret, supremely holy, most excellent, directly enjoyable, attended with virtue, very easy to practise and imperishable – Lord Krishna – BG 9.2.

Our faith is stronger when we see Krishna's photo or idol in front of us at home or in temples. Attunement with the manifest form is achieved easily as we are all body conscious people. However, He is present everywhere, i.e., He is in our heart, He is the guide, mentor, father and witness of everything. He is in everyone. There is nothing that can exist without Him. These forms are un-manifest forms. He has thousands of eyes, ears and He has a face in all directions because He is pervading the universe.

When we get this understanding that He is with us all the time, then we will think of Him all the time and with this inspiration, we do the right Karmas and lift ourselves up. Our goal needs to be the spiritual world Above Time, not a rebirth in the material world which goes up to Brahma Lok (the abode of the creator of this universe) downwards. This is liable to birth and re-birth. Liberation means that we go to the spiritual world. Ties and desires of the material world keep us revolving here and we are here for billions of births. Then this beautiful knowledge of the Bhagavad-Gita comes to us from the Supreme.

This knowledge is most easy to practise, and this tie will not get broken. It is imperishable and immutable. Real happiness lies here, not in material enjoyments.

Knowledge Is Complete When We Know Both Manifest and Un-manifest

मया ततमिदं सर्वं जगदव्यक्तमूर्तिना |

सर्वभूतानि कौन्तेय प्रकृतिं यान्ति मामिकाम् | कल्पक्षये पुनस्तानि कल्पादौ विसृजाम्यहम् ||

प्रकृतिं स्वामवष्टभ्य विसृजामि पुनः पुनः | भूतग्राममिमं कृत्स्नमवशं प्रकृतेर्वशात् ||

The whole of this universe is permeated by Me as Un-manifest Divinity. During the Final Dissolution all beings enter My Prakriti (the prime cause) and at the beginning of creation, I send them forth again. Wielding My Nature I procreate again and again, according to their respective Karmas, all this multitude of beings subject to the sway of their own Nature – Lord Krishna – BG 9.4, 9.7–9.8.

We know how important it is for us to realize the un-manifest form of Krishna. The entire universe is formed by the Un-manifest Divinity.

Now Krishna is explaining what happens when Brahma(Creator) finishes his life of 100 years. We were merging back in Brahma's subtle body during the night and coming back during the day. We also saw that one day is approximately 4.32 billion years on the earth. When Lord Brahma does not exist, we all go to Lord Krishna. This does not mean that we are liberated. It just means that we enter into another storehouse which is Above Time. But when the next universe is created, we come back Below Time and then we start our new birth – it is still according to the Karmas that we had performed. So we see how important is it to watch our Karmas.

We have three forces inside us – our Nature that influences our Karmas, latencies of past Karmas that are directed on us by our Planetary System and Krishna's fragment in us. The first two are negligible forces in front of the infinite Krishna. The Bhagavad-Gita is all about invoking this third force, overruling the first two and reaching the Lord.

Krishna Is All, Krishna Is Everywhere

पिताहमस्य जगतो माता धाता पितामहः |
वेद्यं पवित्रमोङ्कार ऋक्साम यजुरेव च ||
गतिर्भर्ता प्रभुः साक्षी निवासः शरणं सुहृत् |
प्रभवः प्रलयः स्थानं निधानं बीजमव्ययम् ||
तपाम्यहमहं वर्षं निगृह्णाम्युत्सृजामि च |
अमृतं चैव मृत्युश्च सदसच्चाहमर्जुन ||

I am the sustainer and ruler of this universe, its father, mother and grandfather, the one worth knowing, the purifier, the sacred syllable OM and the three Vedas – Rig, Yajur and Sama Veda – Lord Krishna – BG 9.17.

I am the supreme goal, sustainer, lord, witness, abode, refuge, well-wisher seeking no return, origin and end, resting place, storehouse to which all beings return at the time of universal destruction and the imperishable seed – Lord Krishna – BG 9.18.

I radiate heat as the Sun, and hold back as well as send forth showers, Arjuna. I am immortality as well as death; even so, I am being and also non-being – Lord Krishna – BG 9.19.

Krishna Is the Protector

अनन्याश्चिन्तयन्तो मां ये जनाः पर्युपासते |
तेषां नित्याभियुक्तानां योगक्षेमं वहाम्यहम् ||

The devotees, however, who loving no one else constantly think of Me, and worship Me in a disinterested spirit, to those ever united in through with Me, I bring full security and personally attend to their needs – Lord Krishna – BG 9.22.

Those who fall in love with Krishna get protected by Him. On the spiritual path, the person who gets completely absorbed in thoughts of Krishna, Krishna takes care of his security and needs. The Lord is inside us, He is all around us and He is present in everyone around us.

You Reach Where Your Faith Belongs

यान्ति देवव्रता देवान्पितॄन्यान्ति पितृव्रताः |
भूतानि यान्ति भूतेज्या यान्ति मद्याजिनोऽपि माम् ||

Those who are votaries of gods, go to gods, those who are votaries of manes, reach the manes; those who adore the spirits, reach the spirits and those who worship Me, come to Me alone. My devotees are no longer subject to birth and death – Lord Krishna – BG 9.25.

We have gods Below Time and we have gods Above Time. If we worship gods Below Time, then we establish a relationship with them and we reach them after death. Since these gods are Below Time, they are influenced by impact of three Gunas – Sattvik, Rajasic and Tamasic. Once we exhaust the fruits earned because of our merits, we return back to the earth and go through the cycle of birth and death one more time.

If we establish our devotion to the Gods Above Time then, if we are sincere in our devotion, we will reach them after death and since these Gods are Above Time, we will not be reborn. Thus, Lord Krishna tells Arjuna that His devotees are not reborn.

Lord Shiva's Dham is Above Time. Mother Yogamaya or Mahalaxmi is Above Time. Hari Dham, where Lord Narayan resides, is Above Time. Lord Rama's abode is Above Time and Radha–Krishna's abode Golok–Vrindavan, is Above Time. Lord Radha–Krishna have taken various forms Above Time. OM emerges from Lord Krishna. Yogamaya is the spiritual potency of Lord Krishna. She took birth on earth (when Krishna took birth) as the daughter of Nand and Yashoda. So Yogamaya is also the sister of Lord Krishna.

Krishna's Followers Rise on the Spiritual Path and Do Not Fall

पत्रं पुष्पं फलं तोयं यो मे भक्त्या प्रयच्छति ।
तदहं भक्त्युपहृतमश्नामि प्रयतात्मनः ॥
कौन्तेय प्रतिजानीहि न मे भक्तः प्रणश्यति ॥

Whosoever offers Me with love a leaf, a flower, a fruit or water, I appear in person before that selfless devotee of sinless mind, and delightfully partake of that article offered by him with love – Lord Krishna – BG 9.26.

Know it for certain, Arjuna, that My devotee never perishes – Lord Krishna – BG 9.31.

Krishna is in our hearts. He knows everything that we think and do. He is always guiding us and He is our spiritual support. Everything belongs to Him. There is nothing that is ours. He gets pleased with a simple heart and simple offerings. When we develop the Nature of offering everything to Krishna, and also offer all Karmas to Krishna, then we become pure. The Lord accepts everything that we offer with love because He is everywhere; it is just our realization that needs to get firmed up.

Once we go on Lord Krishna's path, He ensures that we are not lost on the spiritual path. He becomes our guide and takes care of us.

Krishna Is All

अहमात्मा गुडाकेश सर्वभूताशयस्थितः ||
आदित्यानामहं विष्णुर्ज्योतिषां रविरंशुमान् | मरीचिर्मरुतामस्मि नक्षत्राणामहं शशी ||
भूतानामस्मि चेतना ||
रुद्राणां शङ्करश्चास्मि ||
गिरामस्म्येकमक्षरम् |यज्ञानां जपयज्ञोऽस्मि ||
रामः शस्त्रभृतामहम् |स्रोतसामस्मि जाह्नवी ||
अध्यात्मविद्या विद्यानां ||
अहमेवाक्षयः कालो धाताहं विश्वतोमुखः ||
मृत्युः सर्वहरश्चाहमुद्भवश्च भविष्यताम् |कीर्तिः श्रीर्वाक्च नारीणां स्मृतिर्मेधा धृतिः क्षमा ||
गायत्री छन्दसामहम् ||
यच्चापि सर्वभूतानां बीजं तदहमर्जुन |न तदस्ति विना यत्स्यान्मया भूतं चराचरम् ||

I am the universal Self seated in the hearts of all beings. I am Vishnu, the radiant Sun among the luminaries, the glow of Maruts, the Moon among the lord of stars. I am consciousness (life-energy) in living beings. Among the eleven Rudras, I am Shiva. I am sacred syllable OM. Among sacrifices, I am the sacrifice of Japa (chanting of holy name). I am Sri Rama, I am the Ganges. Of all knowledge, I am the knowledge of the Soul (metaphysics).

I am verily the endless Time (the devourer of Time – God). I am the sustainer of all, having my face on all sides. I am the all-destroying Death that annihilates all, and the origin of all that are to be born. Of feminities, I am Kirti, Sri, Vak, Smrti, Medha, Dhrti and Ksama (the goddesses presiding over glory, prosperity, speech, memory, intelligence, fortitude and forbearance, respectively). I am the hymn known as Gayatri. I am the seed of all life. For there is no creature, moving or unmoving, which can exist without Me – Lord Krishna – BG 10.20–10.23, 10.25, 10.31–10.35, 10.39.

Krishna's Time Spirit Deals with Karmas of the People

कालोऽस्मि लोकक्षयकृत्प्रवृद्धोलोकान्समाहर्तुमिह प्रवृत्तः |
ऋतेऽपि त्वां न भविष्यन्ति सर्वेऽयेऽवस्थिताः प्रत्यनीकेषु योधाः ||

I am the mighty Kala (the eternal Time-spirit), the destroyer of the worlds. I am out to exterminate these people. Even without you all these warriors arrayed in the enemy's camp shall die – Lord Krishna – BG 11.32.

Even before the Mahabharata battle started, Krishna showed the end of the war to Arjuna. So everything was pre-decided. Arjuna was merely an instrument of God's will. He was chosen for this because of his meritorious latencies of past Karmas. Krishna said, "Among Pandavas, I am Arjuna." So in a way, Krishna also fought the battle not as Krishna but as Arjuna.

This illustrates the theory of Karma. While evil-doers were going to die, even their supporters who were pious were also going to meet the same fate. The lesson from Mahabharata is – while bad Karmas lead to bad destiny, the supporters of those performing bad Karmas also die for supporting the evil-doers.

Worshippers of OM and Krishna Reach the Same Destination

क्लेशोऽधिकतरस्तेषामव्यक्तासक्तचेतसाम् ।
अव्यक्ता हि गतिर्दुःखं देहवद्भिरवाप्यते ॥

The strain is greater for those who have their mind attached to the Un-manifest, as attunement with the Un-manifest is attained with difficulty by the body-conscious people – Lord Krishna – BG 12.5.

This is one of the most important verses of the Bhagavad-Gita as it has a very deep and key message from Lord Krishna. Arjuna asked the question about the destination of people worshipping the Un-manifest (i.e., OM) as against those worshipping the Manifest (Lord Krishna). The Lord explained that worshippers of OM also reach Krishna. This is because the energy of OM emerges from Krishna Himself. The path is different for those worshipping the Un-manifest and those worshipping the Manifest. Krishna advises to worship Him with form because we are all body-conscious people and it is easy for us to tune ourselves with the Lord who is in a form similar to ours. So, while the destination is the same for both the worshippers, the worshippers of OM go through more strain.

In Un-manifest Form He Is All Around Us, Watching Us as the Witness

सर्वतः पाणिपादं तत्सर्वतोऽक्षिशिरोमुखम् ।
सर्वतः श्रुतिमल्लोके सर्वमावृत्य तिष्ठति ॥

He has hands and feet on all sides; eyes, head and mouth in all directions; and ears all-around; for He stands pervading all in the universe – Lord Krishna – BG 13.13.

Lord Krishna's un-manifest form is OM. Un-manifest means that He is not visible to us, as we have material visibility, while our consciousness can cross any boundaries. In His un-manifest form, He is present all around us, listening to us, guiding us, watching us and a witness to what we do. Those who realize His presence all around them are "knowers of Tattva", i.e., knowers of real Him and knowers of real Truth. He is the only Truth, our bodies and this universe is temporary and hence not true. The soul in us, which is His fragment, is the real Truth and is the same as Him because it is His fragment.

As He is all around us, He can change anything in the universe. While He follows His own rules of Karmas, Bhakti and purity can make any change to the latencies of past Karmas.

There Is Only One God; He Appears in Different Forms and Is Present All Around

अविभक्तं च भूतेषु विभक्तमिव च स्थितम् ।
भूतभर्तृ च तज्ज्ञेयं ग्रसिष्णु प्रभविष्णु च ॥

Though integral like space in its undivided aspect, it appears divided as it were, in all animate and inanimate beings. And that Godhead, who is only one worth knowing, is sustainer of beings (as Vishnu), the destroyer (as Rudra) and the creator of all (as Brahma) – Lord Krishna – BG 13.16.

There is only one God but He appears to us in different forms. He is OM as Un-manifest, present all over the universes and in all the filled and empty spaces. To perform His duties, He appears as Creator of the universes. He sustains all the universes and then He destroys the universes and then He re-creates the universes. This cycle has been going for an infinite period and will continue for an infinite period. It has no beginning and it has no end.

Complete God Is Present in Our Hearts

ज्योतिषामपि तज्ज्योतिस्तमसः परमुच्यते |
ज्ञानं ज्ञेयं ज्ञानगम्यं हृदि सर्वस्य विष्ठितम् ||

That supreme Brahma is said to be the light of all lights and entirely beyond Maya. That Godhead is knowledge itself, worth knowing, and worth attaining through real wisdom, and is particularly abiding in the hearts of all – Lord Krishna – BG 13.18.

Continuing from the previous verse, it is further explained that the same Brahma, whom we also call OM, is the light of all lights. While we see light in the Sun and the Moon and light in the wisdom of the wise and light in every atom, the source or energy behind all the light is Brahma. He is the real Godhead. He is the one who is worth knowing as all other knowledge is just a subset of that knowledge. That is why Lord Krishna said that among all the sciences, He is the science of Soul (which is Metaphysics).

Brahma, who is One, appears divided as the creator, sustainer and destroyer of the universes. He is particularly abiding in our hearts. This is the unrealized energy and wisdom that is inside us that we are not able to realize because of the presence of Maya. Maya is basically our desires and negative forces of anger, jealousy, etc. We live in the world of Maya and keep taking birth after birth and never realize the truth. This is the reason for our sufferings for long times that can end if we wish, or they will continue for ever if we do not work on God-realization.

We Migrate to Higher or Lower Worlds Based on Our Deeds as Humans

पुरुषः प्रकृतिस्थो हि भुङ्क्ते प्रकृतिजान्गुणान् ।
कारणं गुणसङ्गोऽस्य सदसद्योनिजन्मसु ॥

Only the Purusha, in association with Prakriti, experiences objects of the Nature of the three Gunas evolved from Prakriti. It is the attachment to these Gunas that is responsible for the birth of this Soul in good and evil wombs – Lord Krishna – BG 13.22.

We are born as Humans. We have a Soul inside that is God and is imperishable and we have our bodies that are perishable. We live in the world of Maya and perform good, bad and mixed activities. These activities are responsible for our next birth in good or evil wombs. There are 8.4 million type of species. Out of 8.4 million, 0.4 million are Human births. There is a lot of difference between one Human and another, and all of them fall into around 400,000 types. All other species of lower Nature behave in the same manner, for example, all tigers behave in the same manner. Similarly, all plants of similar types behave the same, e.g., there is similarity between mango trees. The only birth which is vast is Human birth as that is the gateway where, based on activities, either the Soul migrates to higher worlds or stays in the middle as Human birth or migrates to the lower births. There is no way to reach Krishna from the higher worlds or from the lower worlds. The higher worlds are rewards for our good deeds because we chose the path where we wanted return for our good deeds. But there are no new Karmas there, so we fall back as Humans when the reward for meritorious work is exhausted. Lower worlds are for punishment and we return back to Human birth when the punishment is complete. We need to realize the importance of Human birth.

Our Own Soul Is the Witness and Decides Our Migration to Higher and Lower Worlds

उपद्रष्टानुमन्ता च भर्ता भोक्ता महेश्वरः |
परमात्मेति चाप्युक्तो देहेऽस्मिन्पुरुषः परः ||

The Spirit dwelling in this body, is really the same as the Supreme. He has been spoken of as the Witness, the True Guide, the Sustainer of all, the Experiencer (as the embodied Soul), the Overlord and the Absolute as well – Lord Krishna – BG 13.23.

Who decides on our migration to the higher or the lower worlds? We decide ourselves. There is a Soul inside us which is personal to us and is a fragment of Lord. It is imperishable. Even when all the universes are destroyed, this Soul will stay alive as it will never die. This Soul is witness to everything we think and do and it is this Soul inside us that takes us to different births based on our Karmas.

Like the Sun Lights Up the Solar System, the Soul Lights Our Body with Consciousness

यथा प्रकाशयत्येकः कृत्स्नं लोकमिमं रविः |
क्षेत्रं क्षेत्री तथा कृत्स्नं प्रकाशयति भारत ||

As the Sun illumines this entire universe, so the one Atma (spirit) illumines the whole Ksetra (field or body) – Lord Krishna – BG 13.33.

The Soul has been compared with the Sun. As the Sun illumines the entire Solar system (not just the earth), in the same way, our Soul illumines the complete body, which is our consciousness. We are nothing without this Soul and a body cannot function without this Soul.

Three Gunas: Three Destination after This Birth

यदा सत्त्वे प्रवृद्धे तु प्रलयं याति देहभृत् |
तदोत्तमविदां लोकानमलान्प्रतिपद्यते ||
रजसि प्रलयं गत्वा कर्मसङ्गिषु जायते |
तथा प्रलीनस्तमसि मूढयोनिषु जायते ||

When a man dies during the preponderance of Sattva, he obtains the stainless ethereal worlds (heaven etc.) attained by men of noble deeds. Dying when Rajas predominates, he is born among those attached to action. Even so, the man who has expired during the preponderance of Tamas is reborn in the species of the deluded creatures such as insects and beasts, etc. – Lord Krishna – BG 14.14–14.15.

As we have seen, Lord Krishna said in verse 18.40 that no one in this universe or even the higher worlds of gods is free from the three Gunas. Here the Lord is talking of all existences Below Time, which includes the realm of the creator, Lord Brahma. This covers the complete Solar System. Now what matters is the degree of each Sattva (mode of goodness), Rajas (mode of action) and Tamas (mode of ignorance). All three are present in each individual and gods who exist Below Time.

If Sattva dominates and the person is mostly in the mode of goodness, he will migrate to the higher worlds. If he is always working towards action to fulfil desires, hatred and jealousy, then he is in the middle region, i.e., Human birth and if he is in the mode of sleep, sloth and doing bad to others, he is in the mode of ignorance and headed for lower worlds.

Lord Krishna is above all three. If we always stay in Sattva, we are still destined for worlds Below Time. Lord Krishna's message in the Bhagavad-Gita can take us Above Time.

Krishna Is Substratum of OM

ब्रह्मणो हि प्रतिष्ठाहममृतस्याव्ययस्य च |
शाश्वतस्य च धर्मस्य सुखस्यैकान्तिकस्य च ||

I am the Substratum of the imperishable Brahma, of immortality, of the eternal Dharma and of unending immutable bliss – Lord Krishna – BG 14.27.

This is, again, one of the most beautiful verses with real, deep messages:

Krishna says that He is the Substratum of imperishable Brahma, which means that Brahma or energy of OM emerges from Krishna. That is why Krishna had said in verse 12.4 that devotees of OM or Brahma also reach Him because He is the source.

Lord Krishna blesses immortality and He saves the eternal Dharma which has the real wisdom for the jivas to progress on the spiritual path.

And finally, He is source of immutable bliss. There are things that can be muted. We have seen that Soul cannot be muted. It cannot be cursed by any learned scholar because it is a fragment of Lord Krishna. In the same way, when we worship and do our Karmas, we get blessed by Lord Krishna and no on can mute His blessings. His blessings are the only thing we need in our lives. His blessing stays with us birth after birth and also if we migrate to Lord's Abode.

Krishna's Abode Is Self-illumined

न तद्भासयते सूर्यो न शशाङ्को न पावकः |
यद्गत्वा न निवर्तन्ते तद्धाम परमं मम ||

Neither the Sun nor the Moon nor fire can illumine that supreme self-effulgent state, attaining which they never return to this world; that is My supreme abode– Lord Krishna – BG 15.6.

Lord Krishna explains about His Abode where He resides with Radha and devotees. The place is Above Time so there is no birth-and-death cycles. The place is also self-illumined as Sun is in the Solar system. Once a Soul crosses the timeline, it does not return to the material world. It is free from the evils of the material worlds and bodily pains of old age, disease, birth and death. The Soul is protected by Yogamaya, the spiritual potency of Lord Krishna. Even when these Souls descend to the material worlds with a purpose, they are protected and do not suffer these pains.

Soul Carries Our Mind and Senses to the Next Birth

शरीरं यदवाप्नोति यच्चाप्युत्क्रामतीश्वरः |
गृहीत्वैतानि संयाति वायुर्गन्धानिवाशयात् ||

Even as the wind wafts scents from their seat, so too, the Jivatma, which is the controller of the body etc., taking the mind and the senses from the body which it leaves behind, forthwith migrates to the body which it acquires – Lord Krishna – BG 15.8.

Our Nature moves with us from birth to birth. Our Karmas move with us and become latencies of past Karmas. We are all on a machine that is run by God's system. The machine runs according to our Nature and of past Karmas, though we think we are running the system. It is our ignorance that we think that we are running or influencing the system – we can't do either. We are too small to interfere in His system of fair judgement. We may realize that or ignore that.

Lord Krishna says that when we leave our body, our Soul migrates to another body. The new body depends on our Nature and Karmas. The Soul, while staying pure, carries with itself our mind and our senses. This means that a person who dies as an angry person will be born as an angry person. A person who is very pious by Nature or soft by Nature or always helpful to others will have the same attributes when he moves to the next body.

Individual Is Born with Divine or Demoniac Propensities

दैवी सम्पद्विमोक्षाय निबन्धायासुरी मता ।
मा शुच: सम्पदं दैवीमभिजातोऽसि पाण्डव ॥
द्वौ भूतसर्गौ लोकेऽस्मिन्दैव आसुर एव च ॥

The divine endowment has been recognized as conducive to liberation, and the demoniac one as leading to bondage. Grieve not, Arjuna, for you are born with the divine propensities.

There are only two types of men in this world, the one possessing a divine Nature and the other possessing a demoniac disposition – Lord Krishna – BG 16.5–16.6.

Lord Krishna says that all people are either born with Divine or Demoniac propensities. This message is in line with the earlier messages that the Soul carries the mind and senses along with it and birth happens as per our Karmas. Arjuna was a divine person and was born with divine properties. Lord Krishna had also said that among Pandavas, "I am Arjuna." So the Lord was present in a more shining manner in Arjuna as he exhibited properties that were not equal to but more on the path of Lord Krishna.

We are all born either with Divine properties or Demoniac properties. Accordingly, we continue our journey from the previous births towards liberation or bondage.

Follow the Scriptures Instead of Following Your Own Sweet Will

य: शास्त्रविधिमुत्सृज्य वर्तते कामकारत: ।
न स सिद्धिमवाप्नोति न सुखं न परां गतिम् ॥

Discarding the injunctions of the scriptures, he who acts in an arbitrary way according to his own sweet will, such a person neither attains occult powers, nor the supreme goal, nor even happiness – Lord Krishna – BG 16.23.

We are driven by our Nature. We are basically what our Nature is. All of us have different faiths and beliefs. But that may not be in line with what scriptures say. If we use our own intelligence for spiritual progress and decide ourselves what is right and what is not, we may not reach anywhere.

Hence Lord Krishna advised Arjuna to follow the scriptures; there is no scripture like the Bhagavad-Gita that came from Lord Krishna Himself, with no interpreter in between. It is God's song that is given to us.

OM Is the Un-manifest Form of Krishna and His Other Names Are TAT and SAT

ॐ तत्सदिति निर्देशो ब्रह्मणस्त्रिविधः स्मृतः |
ब्राह्मणास्तेन वेदाश्च यज्ञाश्च विहिताः पुरा ||

OM, TAT and SAT – this has been declared as the triple appellation of Brahma, who is Truth, Consciousness and Bliss. By that were the Brahmanas and the Vedas as well as sacrifices created at the Cosmic Dawn – Lord Krishna – BG 17.23.

In this verse, Krishna describes His un-manifest form, which has been widely understood as OM. Here the Lord says that the un-manifest form has three names – OM, TAT and SAT. Also explained is the Nature of the Un-manifest which is Truth, Consciousness and Bliss. Truth because this is the only Truth which exists everywhere, even in vacuum, besides living and non-living beings. There is nothing where He is not present. Nothing can exist without Him. Consciousness means that He is listening, watching everything and also recording everything. He is also the consciousness which is the Mentor, Father and Mother, always guiding us to perform the right Karmas. He is Bliss means that He is always blessing – even the person who is a criminal, He is blessing and guiding Him to go to the right path. Since the Nature of OM is blessing, this form cannot curse anyone. That is why anyone who has similar Nature like OM gets entitled to go to the Hari Dham of Lord Narayana. The Lord says that this un-manifest form was the principle force behind the creation of this universe and also all the universes that exist. This force created Brahmans and Vedas at the Cosmic Dawn, i.e., when the universe was formed. The universe exists for billions of years before the night sets in. Not to misunderstand – this force is just Krishna's un-manifest form that emerges out of Krishna.

OM Is the Force of Consciousness and Blessing

तस्माद् ॐ इत्युदाहृत्य यज्ञदानतपःक्रियाः |
प्रवर्तन्ते विधानोक्ताः सततं ब्रह्मवादिनाम् ||

Therefore, acts of sacrifice, charity and austerity, as enjoined by sacred percepts, are always commenced by noble persons, used to the recitation of Vedic chants, with the invocation of the divine name OM – Lord Krishna – BG 17.24.

Noble Souls who understand this truth always recite the word of OM before doing any auspicious work. They take the blessings of the un-manifest form of Lord Krishna which is represented as OM. This is practised by many followers of different sects like Arya Samaj. In Sikhism, worshipping of Ek Onkar is also worshipping of OM. Lord Krishna also says in Bhagavad-Gita that in the last minutes of life, one who utters OM reaches the Supreme. The sound of OM resonates in all the universes and in the middle regions because there is nothing that can exist – Sat or Asat – without OM.

TAT Signifies That All Belongs to the Lord: Sought by Seekers of Liberation

तदित्यनभिसन्धाय फलं यज्ञतप:क्रिया: |
दानक्रियाश्च विविधा: क्रियन्ते मोक्षकाङ्क्षिभि:||

With the idea that all this belongs to God, who is denoted by the appellation TAT, acts of sacrifice and austerity as well as acts of charity of various kinds, are performed by the seekers of liberation, expecting no return for them – Lord Krishna – BG 17.24.

Noble Souls who have risen above the desires of the material world, understand that all this is temporary and everything belongs to the Lord. Hence, in the praiseworthy state of mind, they call the Lord as TAT, which means everything belongs to you (the Lord) and what they offer to Him is anyway given by Him and they have nothing to offer. This is the mindset of seekers of liberation. Liberation means rising above this universe and going back to the Godhead, which is Above Time. This universe is Below Time and is in material form. Rising above means going to the spiritual form. There is no material existence there. In Sikhism, the un-manifest form of Lord is also praised as "Wahe-Guru".

SAT Is Praiseworthy and Auspicious

सद्भावे साधुभावे च सदित्येतत्प्रयुज्यते ।
प्रशस्ते कर्मणि तथा सच्छब्दः पार्थ युज्यते ॥
यज्ञे तपसि दाने च स्थितिः सदिति चोच्यते ।
कर्म चैव तदर्थीयं सदित्येवाभिधीयते ॥

The word "Sat" means eternal existence and goodness. O Arjuna, it is also used to describe an auspicious action. Being established in the performance of sacrifice, penance and charity, is also described by the word "Sat." And so any act for such purposes is named "Sat" – Lord Krishna – BG 17.26–17.27.

"SAT" is used to praise the blessing of the Lord and to recognize that the un-manifest form of Lord is truth. This is to praise the Lord, that only the Lord is SAT which means who will always be there and has always been there. SAT is all goodness. Acts of charity and austerity are called SAT as these are all acts of goodness.

In Sikhism, the un-manifest form of Lord is praised as "SATNAM" – Supreme Absolute Truth.

Charity, Sacrifice, Penance: Purifiers for Even the Wise

यज्ञदानतपःकर्म न त्याज्यं कार्यमेव तत् |
यज्ञो दानं तपश्चैव पावनानि मनीषिणाम् ||

Actions based upon sacrifice, charity and penance should never be abandoned; they must certainly be performed. Indeed, acts of sacrifice, charity and penance are purifying even for those who are wise – Lord Krishna – BG 18.5.

Lord Krishna says that all the noble deeds like sacrifice, charity and penance should never be given up even if a person has reached a very high state of spirituality. These acts should always be performed as these acts purify even the wisest people.

Prescribed or Prohibited Actions: Latencies of Past Karmas

अधिष्ठानं तथा कर्ता करणं च पृथग्विधम् ।
विविधाश्च पृथक्चेष्टा दैवं चैवात्र पञ्चमम् ॥
शरीरवाङ्मनोभिर्यत्कर्म प्रारभते नरः ।
न्याय्यं वा विपरीतं वा पञ्चैते तस्य हेतवः ॥
तत्रैवं सति कर्तारमात्मानं केवलं तु यः ।
पश्यत्यकृतबुद्धित्वान्न स पश्यति दुर्मतिः ॥

The body, the doer, the various senses, the many kinds of efforts, and Divine Providence – these are the five factors of action. These five are the contributory factors for whatever action is performed, whether proper or improper, with body, speech or mind. Those who do not understand this regard the Soul as the only doer. With their impure intellects they cannot see things as they are – Lord Krishna – BG 18.14–18.16.

One very important force that acts on us as we perform a prescribed or prohibited action is latencies of past Karmas. We carry our reactions of Karmas with us of the previous births. We may perform certain prohibited actions without our will as these may have been driven from the latencies of past Karmas. While we perform these actions perforce, we are still not free from the reactions of these Karmas because this force also acted on us based on our own previous Karmas. This is the reason that we never get out of this system and this universe comprising of higher, lower and middle regions. These Gunas are Maya.

Even Gods Up to Brahma Lok Are Not Free from the Three Gunas of Maya

न तदस्ति पृथिव्यां वा दिवि देवेषु वा पुनः ।
सत्त्वं प्रकृतिजैर्मुक्तं यदेभिः स्यात्त्रिभिर्गुणैः ॥

No living being on earth or the higher celestial abodes in this material realm is free from the influence of these three modes of Nature – Lord Krishna – BG 18.4.

We are living in a universe that has 14 worlds. Earth is in the middle. The highest is the world of Lord Brahma who is the creator of this universe. All 7 existences above the earth are called Heavenly Abodes. We migrate to these worlds based on the good Karmas that we perform as Human Beings. Only Human Beings can perform Karmas. During our stay in Heavenly Abodes, when the merits are exhausted, we fall back to the earth. In a similar manner, as a result of bad Karmas, Humans migrate to Hellish Planets that are below the earth and then come back to earth after the demerits are exhausted. We have been going through these cycles for millions and millions of years. All these existences are Below Time.

Lord Krishna says that all the gods and celestial abodes (Heavenly Planets) that we worship within these 14 worlds are also impacted by the three Gunas and even they are not free of them. So worshipping them cannot take us out of the cycles of birth and death around the 14 worlds.

We Should Perform All Our Duties, Even If There Is Some Inbuilt Evil

सहजं कर्म कौन्तेय सदोषमपि न त्यजेत् ।
सर्वारम्भा हि दोषेण धूमेनाग्निरिवावृताः ॥

One should not abandon duties born of one's Nature even if one sees defects in them, O son of Kunti. Indeed, all endeavours are veiled by some evil, as fire is by smoke – Lord Krishna – BG 18.18.

We are all bound by our duties and all our duties have some inbuilt negatives that cannot be avoided. Arjuna, in performing his duty as a Kshatriya (warrior), was expected to kill thousands of people on the opposite side. He was expected to fight this un-solicited and righteous war for the sake of civilians who were facing the pain of an unruly kingdom. He was chosen by God's system to perform this duty based on his merits and latencies of his past Karmas. He cannot abandon this duty even when he knows that there will be a lot of bloodshed. We have to focus on the righteous Karmas and our natural duties while we need to surrender to the Lord for the fruits of our actions.

Our Nature, Latencies and God's Wishes Collectively Act on Us

यदहङ्कारमाश्रित्य न योत्स्य इति मन्यसे |
मिथ्यैष व्यवसायस्ते प्रकृतिस्त्वां नियोक्ष्यति ||

If, motivated by pride, you think, "I shall not fight", your decision will be in vain. Your own material (Kshatriya) Nature will compel you to fight – Lord Krishna – BG 18.59.

We are influenced by our Nature. Our Nature depends on, basically, the dominant Guna of the three Gunas that act on us all the time. We have our Soul which carries the latencies of the past Karmas that act on us. Finally, there is the Oversoul or Krishna talking to our Soul, which is also His fragment, all the time. So in a way, we are not always free to perform the actions in the manner we want at a particular moment.

Lord Krishna cautioned to Arjuna that even if he (Arjuna) decided not to fight, his Nature as a warrior and the need to do the righteous acts will force him to fight. So Arjuna should get rid of his ego so that he could decide what to do. Everything was not in his hands.

Our Nature, Latencies and God's Wishes Collectively Act on Us

स्वभावजेन कौन्तेय निबद्ध: स्वेन कर्मणा |
कर्तुं नेच्छसि यन्मोहात्करिष्यस्यवशोऽपि तत् ||

That action, too, which you are not willing to undertake through ignorance you will perforce perform, bound by your own duty born of your Nature – Lord Krishna – BG 18.60.

Krishna told Arjuna that he was not willing to take part in the war out of ignorance. The Lord also told him that even then "you will perforce perform". Here the Lord showed to Arjuna that the decision of not fighting was not in his hands. If Arjuna thought that he could take that decision, then he was thinking from his ego and out of ignorance.

Arjuna had been selected to perform the actions of fighting the war due to the merit of his past Karmas. It was God's system and God's wish that had selected Arjuna to perform these actions.

We Are All Mounted on a Machine and Our Past Karmas Run This Machine

ईश्वरः सर्वभूतानां हृद्देशेऽर्जुन तिष्ठति |
भ्रामयन्सर्वभूतानि यन्त्रारूढानि मायया ||

Arjuna, God abides in the heart of all creatures, causing them to revolve according to their Karma by His illusive power (Maya) as though mounted on a machine – Lord Krishna – BG 18.61.

We are all mounted on a machine and we run as per the instructions of that machine. This machine works based on our own Karmas of the past. This machine is run by God's system which is called here as "Maya". We see small children sitting on a merry-go-round with a steering wheel in their hands. They think they are driving the merry-go-round but actually there is a machine that is driving. Our state is same. It is our past Karmas that are driving us today and it will be our today's Karmas that will drive us in the future.

Karmas become the key. We have to excel in the current environment while still under the influence of past Karmas. But the difficulty is that whatever we do, we will still remain inside the universe of 14 lokas which are all Below Time. Right Karmas and surrender to God and His grace, will show us the exit path.

Take Refuge in Krishna, His Grace Will Give Peace

तमेव शरणं गच्छ सर्वभावेन भारत |
तत्प्रसादात्परां शान्तिं स्थानं प्राप्स्यसि शाश्वतम् ||

Take refuge in Him alone with all your being, Arjuna. By His mere grace you will attain supreme peace and the eternal abode – Lord Krishna – BG 18.62.

In the usual course, there is no way for us to get out from the current existences and reach God's Abode which is Above Time. Our Nature and our Karmas have kept us here for billions of years. In that darkness, Lord Krishna revealed the Bhagavad-Gita 5,000 years ago and gave us the way to reach His Abode.

Krishna is the Oversoul and our Soul is His fragment. To break the bonds of these universes, we need to depend on Krishna and we need His grace. In the end, it is only His grace that will liberate us; our efforts alone will not. His grace will come when we follow the teachings of the Bhagavad-Gita.

Krishna's Grace Will Liberate Us

मच्चित्तः सर्वदुर्गाणि मत्प्रसादात्तरिष्यसि |
अथ चेत्त्वमहङ्कारान्न श्रोष्यसि विनङ्क्ष्यसि ||

With your mind devoted to Me, you shall, by My grace overcome all difficulties. But, if from self-conceit you do not care to listen to Me, you will be lost – Lord Krishna – BG 18.58.

Devotion to Krishna and depending on Him will remove all obstacles so that we can pursue the path to His Abode. Our efforts alone will not work. We need to depend on the Lord and we need to receive His grace.

Krishna's Promise to Devotees

सर्वधर्मान्परित्यज्य मामेकं शरणं व्रज ।
अहं त्वां सर्वपापेभ्यो मोक्षयिष्यामि मा शुच: ॥

Resigning all your duties to Me, the all-powerful and all supporting Lord, take refuge in Me alone; I shall absolve you of all sins, worry not – Lord Krishna – BG 18.66.

Arjuna was a warrior. The Lord asks Arjuna to surrender to Lord and then fight the war. Doing so Arjuna will not incur any sin while performing his duties. The Lord will also remove all his past sins. Once a person is completely purified, he can exit from this universe which is Below Time and which has sufferings of birth, death, old age and disease. The Lord revealed the secrets of existence of the worlds Above Time, which are spiritual worlds where there is no suffering. This verse applies to all of us who are able to surrender to the Lord and offer all our Karmas to the Lord.

मा शुच: – The Lord says, worry not, fear not. This is for the devotees who are on the path of Lord Krishna.

श्रद्धावाननसूयश्च शृणुयादपि यो नर: ।
सोऽपि मुक्त: शुभाँल्लोकान्प्राप्नुयात्पुण्यकर्मणाम् ॥

The person who listens to the holy Gita with reverence, being free from malice, he too, liberated from sin, shall reach the propitious worlds of the virtuous – Lord Krishna – BG 18.71.

Such is the power of the Bhagavad-Gita and such are the blessings of Lord Krishna.

Other Books by the Authors

978 81 207 6658 7

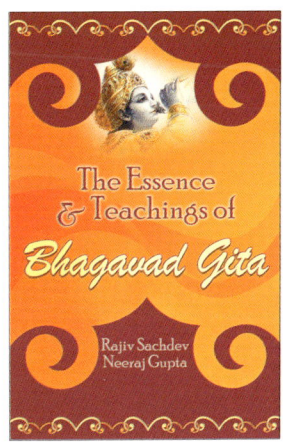

978 81 207 8982 1

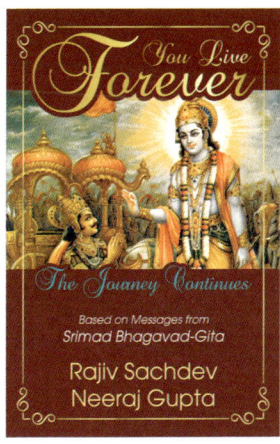

978 81 207 9962 2

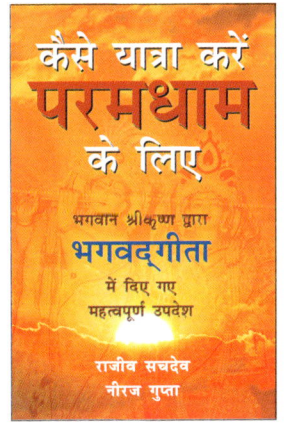

978 81 207 8318 3

978 81 207 8986 8

Books on Spirituality by STERLING

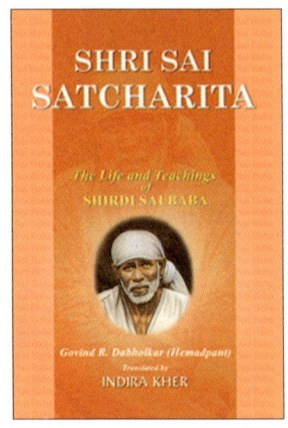

978 81 207 2211 8 (HB)
978 81 207 2153 1 (PB)

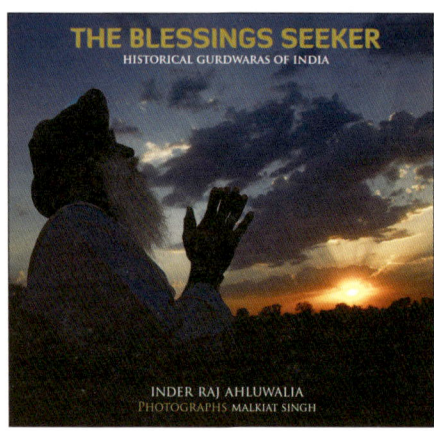

978 93 86245 74 8

978 81 207 5343 3

978 81 207 2524 9

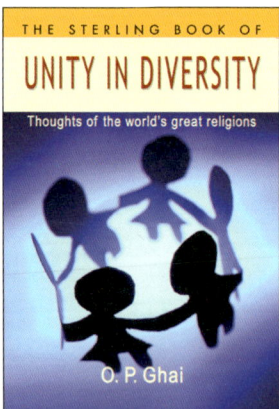

978 81 207 3739 6

mail@sterlingpublishers.in   www.sterlingpublishers.in